CHINESE
IMMIGRANT
COOKING

CHINESE
IMMIGRANT
COOKING

BY MARY TSUI PING YEE

Food Photography by Bill Yenne

FIRST GLANCE BOOKS

Cobb, California

Published by First Glance Books, Inc.

© 1998 O.G. Publishing Corp.

Distributed by First Glance Books, Inc.
PO Box 960
Cobb, CA 95426
Phone: (707) 928-1994, Fax: (707) 928-1995

Produced by American Graphic Systems, Inc.
PO Box 460313
San Francisco, CA 94146
Fax: (415) 285-8790

Design © 1998 American Graphic Systems, Inc.

ISBN 1-885440-32-4
Printed in Hong Kong

Food Photographer: Bill Yenne
Food Coordinator and Stylist: Melinda Israel
Head Cook: Nam Singh
Assistant Cooks: Sandra Woolf, Melinda Israel and
Cora Maevon Chun
Props: Melinda Israel and Cora Maevon Chun
Photographer's Assistants: Azia Yenne and Lisa Yenne

Note: The Chinese transliteration given for names of
recipes and foods in this book are efforts by Mary
Israel (Mary Tsui Ping Yee) to render her parents'
dialect of Cantonese.

Special thanks to the following individuals for the use
of props and for their assistance:
Mr. and Mrs. Edward Tom, Jennie Horn, Alva Scott
Parnow, Sandy Wong, Sue Lim Yee, Nam Singh,
Andrew Martin Porcelain, San Rafael, CA, Asian
Market, San Rafael, CA, Dea Conrath, Cora Maevon
Chun, Sandra Woolf, Kathleen Lustman.

Designed by Bill Yenne with design assistance from
Azia Yenne. Proofreading by Joan B. Hayes.

All food photography © Bill Yenne

All other photographs are from the personal collec-
tions of Mary Israel and Ann Tom, with the following exceptions:
Stock Editions: page 130
© Azia Yenne: pages 40, 42, 46, 48, 60, 78, 104
© Bill Yenne: pages 2, 8-9, 21, 24, 79, 101, 105, 126
top & bottom, 137, 180, 190-191, 192

Top: Barbecue Pork Buns. Above: Watercress Soup.

DEDICATION

I wish to pay tribute to the memory of my parents, whose lives have inspired my personal and professional interest in the history and culture of China. Putting these recipes and stories in print is a small measure of appreciation for all their teachings to me about food and family.

In addition, this book would not have been possible without the many friends and family members who have eaten at my table and who have entertained me at their meals. These include members of my family who shared their memories with me, in particular my sisters Ann and Jennie who contributed their favorite family recipes and treasured family photos for this book. I also dedicate this book to my daughters Melinda and Tania, who have gladdened a mother's heart by continuing our tradition of home cooking, and especially to Melinda for persuading me to undertake this project, and for her artistic direction for the photographs of my recipes. Also, for the food preparation, Nam Singh receives my appreciation for his invaluable help.

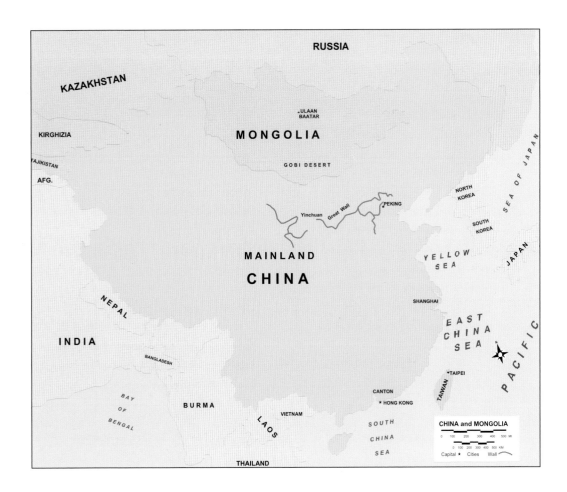

CONTENTS

(Illustration at top: see page 94. Illustration overleaf: Chinatown in San Francisco as it appears now.)

FOREWORD

BY MELINDA ISRAEL

When my mother, Mary Tsui Ping Yee, cooks, she draws on generations of passed-down wisdom, from our ancestral village in Guangdong, where my grandparents were born, from her childhood home in America, and from her many travels in modern day China. There is a spirit in her cooking that has come down from mother to daughter, a legacy I received as well; standing by her side as her cleaver rendered vegetables into bite-sized pieces, the bowls of measured soy sauce and wine, the alchemy as each element was added and expertly swirled into the blackened surface of the wok, until the perfect moment for consumption—a moment learned as much by intuition as technique.

It's a sight and a taste I never forget—and, as she has taught me, the first step in learning great Chinese home cooking is training the taste buds on lovingly prepared cuisine, such as she served to my family as I grew up, just as her mother cooked for her.

These lessons for me took place in our home in a small city in central Virginia. Like my mother's childhood in Canonsburg, Pennsylvania, we were far from any relatives, or even any other Chinese. But our house, a brick, colonial style home with scrolls of calligraphy on the walls, filled with Oriental carpets and souvenirs from my parents' many travels, was a bastion of Chinese culture and cuisine, a fact I really only appreciated once I had grown up.

As a child, I took for granted the delicious meals we enjoyed every night at our kitchen table, such as my mother's superb Oyster Beef and Broccoli (page 64) or summer feasts on the back porch. For these my mother might mari-

Above: This is a favorite family photograph of me with my mother and father and my sister Tania.

nate her Chinese style barbecued chicken (page 116) or flank steak (page 64) and my father would cook it up on the outdoor grill. I'm sure the smells wafting over the fence made our neighbors envious! To this day, even after traveling to Beijing itself, I have never tasted a duck that compares with the crispiness and perfection of my mother's Christmas dinners with Peking duck (page 120).

My mother has a knack for taking whatever is handy and making a delicious innovation with it—a creative adaptability that she attributes to Cantonese cooking altogether. Often, we would enjoy freshly picked eggplant or beans from my father's ever-growing vegetable garden. "A pinch of sugar and a pinch of salt," my mother would tell me, as she dropped the seasonings into the sizzling wok. Coming home from school in the spring, I might be greeted by a house filled with the starchy smell of freshly canned bamboo. My mother would put old coffee cans upside down over the new shoots in the backyard, so that their skins would stay white and tender in the darkness until they were big enough to harvest. The large grove of beautiful bamboo behind the house, which swayed and rustled in the wind, or bowed in the winter under the white weight of snow, was one of the reasons my parents were attracted to the house originally.

Because our extended family was far away, it was my parents' many friends and visitors who benefited from my mother's excellent cuisine. I remember the elegant parties where guests oohed and ahhed over platters of succulent meats and exotic flavors—events my mother would prepare for days in advance. I also remember sitting at the top of the stairs with my sister (well after our bedtime!)

and peeking through the banisters at the spectacle of one of my mother's "Cantonese Fire Pot" parties. The fire pot, with its tall, copper chimney for the smoking charcoal, and moat for heating water, stayed in its place of honor on top of the carved china cabinet until such occasions, when it was lovingly polished and filled for guests to dip and cook their little baskets of meats. I'm sure for its time (and even now!) it was the most exotic "fondue" south of the Mason-Dixon!

The fire pot was actually not a dish from my mother's childhood, but from her years living in Taiwan before I was born. My parents were scholars of Asian studies, which took them to many places. In fact, when mainland China became open to American travelers in 1979, my mother's credentials in Asian studies from Stanford and Harvard made her the perfect tour leader for the Smithsonian Institution. It was natural, then, when dishes and flavors from her many overseas banquets began appearing on our table at home.

As you can tell, my parents were true gourmets and they taught us how to appreciate good food by eating well whether it was leftovers from the fridge, crab we caught on our camping trips to North Carolina, or sampling noodle shops

Above: This is a picture of me with my mother and grandmother in our house when I was about three.
Below: My mother, sister Tania and I have just finished building a Chinese snowman in our back yard in Virginia.

in Taiwan. One secret that you would never know from reading my mother's recipes is that she is an all-around incredible cook—no matter what the cuisine! At our dinner table, she was just as likely to be serving coq au vin or moussaka as stir-fried shrimp! (Guests, however, would be served only Chinese food since my mother soon learned they would be disappointed otherwise!) And my father, a Jewish New Yorker, always made sure visitors from the North packed fresh loaves of rye bread in their suitcases for their visit to our home.

In this "melting wok" of a culture we were beneficiaries of an incredible palate of fine cooking—a true gift of the American immigrant experience. But among all these legacies, the food of my maternal grandmother, called "Po Po" by her grandchildren, was a direct link for me to the living Chinese tradition of good cooking.

By the time I got to know her, Po Po lived in San Francisco, and it was so far away we visited her only a few times when I was a child. Sadly, my grandfather had died when I was about five, so I know him best through all the stories my mother and my aunts tell about him. But our visits to Po Po's Hyde Street apartment house will forever be clear in my mind and on my palate!

Po Po spoke only a little English, but her communication to her two non-Chinese-speaking grandchildren was in a universal language: food! We would barley reach the top of her steep apartment stairs when she would appear, warm and welcoming in her housecoat, head full of tight, grey curls framing a beaming smile. "You want some . . . cookie cake candy?" The signs of her love came in pink boxes from Chinatown bakeries, filled with our favorite steamed buns, bags of fortune cookies, and as many sweet sesame candies as we could eat! I will never forget when my parents left us in her care for several days and my sister Tania and I were at that "picky stage" of eating. Not a problem with Po Po—she served us our favorite dish—chicken and cashew nuts—every single night until our parents returned! Another true sign to us of her love.

We would spend hours sitting with her in the front room, where below the bay windows cable cars churned, clanging up the hill. Despite the language barrier, she liked to watch American TV—her favorites were the shows that must have reminded her of the exaggerated plots and acro-batics of Chinese entertainment: television soap operas and all star wrestling! While she watched from the nubby brown sofa, her fingers were busy knitting fantastic creations from many colors of yarn—especially pink. These cardigans, doilies for the furniture, and even crocheted flowers she made by following no instructions at all, and were bestowed on us all in her unending generosity.

Her house was decorated in the traditional Chinese style, full of bowls of fruit—bright oranges and apples, many flowering plants and greenery, all signs of good luck and prosperity. Her airy kitchen in the rear of the apartment had a long Formica-topped table where we'd eat every day, then there was a round table in the stairwell for when the larger family was there—as many of my many aunts, uncles and cousins as could make it for her incredible feasts.

For these occasions, an outrageous abundance of dishes would appear from her kitchen, to the point where we all had to repeatedly refuse any more of the helpings urged upon us. Here, at my grandmother's table, is where I learned the unwritten rules of the Chinese dinner table:

Left: Here are my sister and Tania and I saying "good night" to Po Po on her sofa during a visit

1. As a hostess it is your duty to serve more than anyone could ever possibly eat.

2. No matter how much your guests refuse, you continue to heap further helpings on their plate until they can barely manage a nibble.

3. As the guest in a Chinese home, leaving food behind in your rice bowl is a mandatory sign of good manners, showing that you have been more than well fed!

Here, too, is where I witnessed my grandmother's love for my mother — and her love in return. Of course, it was in the form of food! At one time or another, my grandmother had gotten the idea that my mother's favorite food was that great delicacy of Chinese cuisine: sea slug soup!

So every time we visited her house she would specially bring home the best dried sea slug in Chinatown, soak it for a day, and then cook it for almost as long, to get the rubbery texture out of it. Then, and always, at least once during our stay, it would appear, floating in a broth (and perfectly prepared), in honor of her oldest daughter's rare visit. What my grandmother didn't know was that my mother didn't care for sea slug soup at all! But in the true Chinese way, rather than reject her mother's special gift, she dutifully ate it and praised its delicate flavor. Chinese expressions of love may be more subdued than other cultures,' but they are nonetheless powerful and persevering.

My mother tells me, when she sets about making a dish from her past, her memory of the sight, texture and flavor is so vivid she keeps experimenting until it's just right—and then adds the magic touch of her own! In helping my mother compile this cookbook, I was reminded of the great treasure she and my grandmother have given me. May you add your distinct flavor to these recipes and treasure them as much as I do.

Top: My cousin Cathy, Tania and I on the steps of Po Po's building. Right: My mother and I wok-cooking one of her recipes for this book.

INTRODUCTION

Some of my happiest memories of growing up in Canonsburg, Pennsylvania are associated with the meals my mother cooked every day. A Chinese hand laundry is an unlikely setting for great food, but for 18 years I thrived on dishes that had the authentic flavor and variety of the best Cantonese cooking. In my adult life, I've tasted fine cuisine in many places, but for food that pleases the palate and warms the heart, I'll always prefer the home-cooked meals of my childhood.

I was born in 1933 during the Great Depression—my mother called it "the year all the banks closed." I was not aware of the hard times. In that small town where we were the only Chinese, my parents created a secure life for their close-knit family, which expanded to six children. I learned to speak their dialect of Cantonese before English, to use chopsticks before fork and knife, and to show respect to elders and responsibility for younger sisters before the precepts of Sunday school.

I remember playing under the ironing tables while both Father and Mother worked at the demanding tasks of washing, ironing, and wrapping the laundry.

Until I was almost seven, the laundry location included a backyard where we raised vegetables. I clearly recall standing on stubby 4-year-old legs helping to weed and water rows of bok choy, long beans, and squash. One afternoon I picked a tempting tomato at eye level on the vine and bit into the warm ripeness, letting the juice drip onto my clean pinafore. I wasn't scolded for soiling my clothes.

Above: This is my mother when she first got married.

Mother said, "It should have been washed first!" She didn't trust unpeeled fruit or unboiled tap water, either.

On the boundary of our yard with that of a small farm stood an apple tree which we harvested every fall. A favorite family tale recalls one apple-picking during which I was being chased by the neighbor's pet crow. My father, up in the tree gathering fruit, aimed an apple at the bird and hit my older brother instead. The punch line: "Tom only rubbed his head, but Mary was doing all the crying!"

My parents were the most important people in my world. I thought my father could do anything. He wasn't very tall, but he was very muscular. I would shout in delight as he lifted his arms easily with two of us hanging on either side. He had been educated in the Confucian classics, but proved himself a successful businessman. By the time he retired, he not only owned property but had put all of his children through college. "Study, and make use of what you learn!" he said, and was the best example of brains and energy put to good use. I would proudly hold his tools for him as he built partitions or repaired the laundry machinery; at other times he let me grind the ink for his Chinese brush writing. He worked so hard for his family, but he also knew how to enjoy life. I remember his hearty laughter at jokes, his singing while he ironed shirts, and his teasing as he played a tough game of checkers with me.

Father had arrived in the United States in 1922. The immigration laws of that period made it impossible for him to send for my mother until 1931. During that long separation, Mother had put up with an overbearing older sister-in-law and had to do much of the cooking and childcare in that extended household. When they were finally reunited, she became an equal partner in the business. She was always the first to rise in the morning to start breakfast.

Her feet often hurt from the long hours of standing, but she said, "At least they were never bound, or they'd hurt more!" Father would get a laugh by imitating the swaying totter of a lady with "golden lotus" feet. Mother was always a bit sensitive about the size of her feet, but I remember once when she showed me the gift Father had presented her when she finally arrived—her first pair of high-heeled shoes. I thought it so romantic that she had kept them long after she had outgrown them.

Mother was very outspoken, freely expressing her opinion and feelings. She also told vivid tales of village life; my favorite was about Third Cousin being bitten by a wildcat. While telling of celebrations, "I was one of the women making pastries for the last clan wedding."She would go on with a list of ingredients and descriptions of how they made tray after tray of steamed goodies for the festive banquet. My mouth would water as I listened.

Her capable hands were constantly in motion—adding

Below: This was our family portrait, taken in Canonsburg, Pennsylvania, back in the fall of 1941. From left to right it's me, Ethel, mother, father, Ann and Tom.

starch to freshly laundered shirts, sewing a tiny baby dress, showing me cat's cradle patterns with a bit of string, or deftly slicing a squash into uniform shapes. As the oldest girl, I became the chief apprentice in the kitchen, urged to imitate what she did. I watched her stir-frying some greens: Her motions were a ballet of efficiency—a drizzle of oil from an enamel spout, a few swoops of the spatula, stirring as the other hand adds a pinch of salt and a dash of sauce, then all scooped into the serving dish. No waste

Above: This is Tom and I in our yard in Canonsburg one winter while we were growing up.

of time or fuel, but the vegetables were just the right texture of tender crispness. She didn't measure her ingredients, but she said, "Listen to the sizzle of the oil, look for the color of the meat or vegetables, don't over-season, but just bring out the natural sweetness!"

This style of cooking, the chief characteristic of my parents' native province of Guangdong, demands fresh-ness in what is cooked. The subtropical region of south-east China provides year-'round produce, two crops of rice, and abundant seafood. Mother had to adjust to the cooler climate of western Pennsylvania. This brought out another feature of Cantonese cooking—adaptability and innovation. This region had early on adopted foreign imports—from the curry of India and the fish pastes of southeast Asia to New World corn, potatoes, and squash.

My parents followed this tradition of adapting the produce of their new home to the flavors of the old. Mother always put her unique stamp on anything she cooked. I remember when she cooked a Halloween pump-kin into a colorful dish with dried shrimp. Her Thanksgiv-ing turkey steamed with fermented bean curd was far more moist and more delicious than any roasted gobbler. She, like all Cantonese cooks, took pride in her creative variations. Day in and day out, she cooked meals that were tasty, nutritious, and never boring.

After we moved to the new laundry location, we no longer had a garden. We depended upon local supplies of fresh produce, supplemented by shopping trips to the Chinese grocery in Pittsburgh, an hour's trolley ride away. I also remem-ber occasional crates of vegeta-bles from a New Jersey truck farm, from which I helped to unpack Chinese mustard greens, large white radishes, bumpy, green bitter melon, and silk squash (luffa)—all of which would appear on the table in various dishes in the following days. Father did most of the shopping for groceries, coming home with some ham or spareribs, a bunch of broccoli or beets, and my parents would talk over the menu. Mother might say, "It's getting colder, time for a hearty soup." Father might suggest, "How about garlic and black bean spareribs?" They were partners in every aspect of family life, whether work or nutrition.

Mother produced her daily meals with very simple equipment. A double sink stood near the chopping block, which was a hardwood tree section. The refrigerator, which had replaced the icebox of the old laundry, had a freezing compartment just big enough for the ice cube trays. The stove had several gas burners, but no oven, as baking was not part of Cantonese home-cooking. A steamer, a 14-inch wok, and several pots—with these Mother cooked thousands of meals, and from her kitchen wafted wonderful smells which drove out the lingering laundry odors of starch and bleach.

The dining table was a central piece of furniture. This sturdy, square surface was where I did my homework with the rest of the children. Covered with a cheerful green and white oilcloth, it was where I wrapped neat bundles of laundry in brown paper. But I best remember it as the center of our family meals, with plenty of room for each of us in our own spot. We filled our own rice bowls

and helped ourselves to the dishes placed in the middle of the table. Meals were happy occasions—no scolding or unpleasant topics—where I learned about my parents' approach to enjoying food. If Father commented, "This fish is really fresh," or "The winter melon soup is too salty," Mother would take note because she respected his opinions about food preparation. He had the impulse of a gourmet, always willing to try a new dish. Having worked as an apprentice cook to earn passage money to the States, he enjoyed experimenting with regional dishes.

Father's cooking projects usually took place on Sundays after church. I was only a five-year-old onlooker when he brought home a live tortoise to make into a soup

laced with some of his home-made wine. He had picked up the distilling technique during the years of Prohibition, when such alcoholic products couldn't be bought. I was old enough to help when he attempted the famous shark's fin soup. The triangular fin was soaked and boiled alternately until soft enough for me to help pick out the translucent slivers from the spiny structure. The slight crunchiness of these slivers is the delicacy so much prized in this rich broth. Special dishes often came with celebrations, and every occasion was an excuse for a meal with family and friends. Food was always a part of festivity, whether it was the end of the workweek or a family reunion.

Top: A postcard from Canonsburg. This is how it looked when I lived there. Below: A family portrait: Me, Tom and Ethel in the back row. Ann, Margaret and Jennie are in the front with mother and father.

Above: This is the market in Chinatown that mother and father operated when they moved to San Francisco in 1957.
Below: Here I am at my graduation from Stanford University in California with my friend Alice, my brother Tom and father.

When Cantonese greet each other, they don't ask, "How are you?" but "Have you eaten *fan* (rice) yet?" In our home, rice was the mainstay of any true meal. All of the other dishes were regarded as accompaniments to this essential grain. We children were told to finish the rice in our bowls, for farmers had worked too hard to produce it for us to waste any. I was only eight when I was first given the task of preparing the family rice. First, the rice was rinsed in several changes of water, the impurities carefully picked out, and then the water for cooking the rice covered the grains by an amount I measured with my thumb. At mealtime, a half hour was enough to cook it to fluffy doneness. Our rice came in 100-pound sacks. Once, during the war, supplies of rice ran out for several weeks. My mother was disconsolate. As she set down platters of potatoes, bread, or noodles, she sighed, "*Moh fan haek* (No rice to eat)." What she meant was, "This is really not a meal; without rice, it's only a snack!"

Desserts were not a part of our meals; sweets were classified as snacks. I always looked forward to mid-afternoon snacks from Mother when I got home from school. It might be a carefully-peeled apple or pear, a hand-shaped rice ball with a bit of meat inside, a boiled sweet potato in winter, or a reheated bun or New Year's pudding. Father was always looking for special treats—I remember the fresh coconut he found in the market: We each had a sip of the juice before he cracked the shell with a hammer. The sweet white meat was eaten with honeyed ginger slices. He would

return from shopping expeditions in Pittsburgh with all sorts of packages, which I eagerly opened, hoping to find the sweet-tart plum wafers which came in rolls, crunchy sesame seed candy, or the rich cookies formed from ground nuts. Then my sisters and I would fight over whose turn it was to keep the green boxes that held bundles of herbs.

The bottles of condiments and dried produce went into Mother's larder. This dark wood cupboard was full of wonderful smells. She packed away the herbs which would go into tonic soups, and lined up the bottles of soy sauce, sesame oil, oyster sauce, rice wine, and vinegar.

Above: A photo taken of me at Harvard in 1956.

There were jars of fermented tofu and black bean, shrimp paste and malt sugar. A salty sea smell came from the shelf of dried shrimp, squid, oysters, and scallops. Containers held dried mushrooms, lily buds, lotus root, gingko nuts, and cellophane noodles. From this store of ingredients, she provided the authentic flavors of her native home-cooking and spiced the winter fare of her adopted land.

In my parents' view, food and health were vitally linked. If the balance of elements — "heating" or "cooling" foods — was not matched with the seasons, then illness was more likely. I think our low-fat, high vegetable diet also contributed to the family's well-being. I did enjoy the "comfort" food Mother cooked when I came down with a cold. She would make me a hot bowl of rice *juk* (congee, or gruel) topped by a poached egg, green onions and a bit of oyster sauce for seasoning. It went down very smoothly past a sore throat. Chewing a piece of ginger effectively cleared a stuffy nose. She had all sorts of restoring soups and spring tonics "to clear the system."

Mother never stopped watching over my health and well-being. She would rise early to prepare a rice meal for me before I headed off on my three-day train ride to

college. I was sent off with a heavily-packed basket of chicken, boiled eggs, steamed buns, and fruit — enough to last the whole trip with plenty to spare for fellow passengers! When I married and lived elsewhere, I would get care packages of dried mushrooms, or moon cakes and New Year's red envelopes with money inside. When my parents moved the family to San Francisco in 1957, I looked forward to going there for reunions, which always featured feasts of Mother's wonderful food. The big, round top would enlarge the table so that more than a dozen — young and old — could sit around the many dishes which filled most of the surface.

Mother continued to try out new ways of preparing food. She still insisted upon the freshest of ingredients, and she would walk the eight blocks to the Chinatown markets to pick out the best fish or duck, the freshest greens or tenderest ginger root; back she would walk, carrying two full shopping bags.

She loved cooking for the family and encouraged us to invite our friends along. How she would beam as we would heap compliments on her dishes and serve ourselves more helpings! She doted on her grandchildren, especially after all of her own children had grown up and she lived alone. She kept special jars of snacks for their visits, knit them warm sweaters, and looked forward to keeping them well-fed.

The indelible memory of my parents, and especially of their legacy of home-cooking as an important part of the good life, has inspired me to follow their example. I can feel my mother's guiding spirit as I use my cleaver, mix a sauce, or stir-fry a dish she used to make; I can sense my father's approving smile every time I bone a duck or attempt a new way of spicing eggplant. They are present at every festive meal I enjoy with family and friends. To them I dedicate this book.

COOKING AND SEASONING TECHNIQUES

When I was a child, Canonsburg was indisputably a one-wok town. Beyond our household other families ate entirely different meals, and unless we visited Chinese friends and relatives, the only Cantonese food to be found was what we cooked ourselves. During my lifetime, I have been delighted by the ever-widening popularity of Chinese cuisine and the introduction of wok and cleaver into American kitchens. The term "stir-fry" is now a standard cooking term, and once exotic Chinese ingredients and condiments—water chestnuts, giant white radishes, bean sprouts, taro, bok choy, Napa cabbage, dried mushrooms, sesame oil, soy sauce, fermented black bean, hoisin and oyster sauce — are often stocked in supermarkets.

Moreover, a health-conscious public has come to appreciate the benefits of a low-fat, non-dairy, high-fiber Chinese diet based upon rice or noodles, lots of vegetables, and very little meat. The great variety of savory dishes make it a delightful way to stay healthy without sacrificing flavor. Once having tasted authentic Chinese cuisine (not the fare of ordinary take-outs or frozen food sections) in travel to Asia or at the increasing number of fine Chinese restaurants in this country, many Americans are eager to incorporate these dishes into their own home-cooked meals. Certainly, having grown up with this style of food preparation and eating, my palate is forever attuned to its unique characteristics.

Fortunately, the principles of Chinese cooking are not beyond the ordinary cook. Millions of Chinese have developed these efficient techniques over millennia, and in the modern kitchen, a little practice will result in tasty dishes. The home cook has an advantage over the restaurants, for it is easier to avoid the double-frying which produces extra crispness in steam table buffets, but loads on extra calories. It is also possible to control the amount of salt and other ingredients for special diets.

The most common techniques used in the Cantonese kitchen are moist-heating: boiling, braising and especially steaming. Stir-frying, a method in which the Cantonese excel, has the advantage of speedy cooking with a minimum of oil. Both the nutritional value and the texture of the ingredients are preserved with a saving of fuel and oil. This method requires the cutting of ingredients into thin or small, uniform pieces. My mother seldom deep-fried her dishes, for she considered it too "heating," and also wasteful of cooking oil. The exceptions were usually special dishes for guests or for celebrations. Since the traditional kitchen did not include an oven, roasted meats were usually purchased at a specialty shop or prepared in pits at village barbecues.

In my modern kitchen, I have all sorts of appliances to speed the preparation of dishes: blender, grinder, oven, even a microwave (used mainly to reheat leftovers). However, my basic tools are still a wok, a chopping block, and a cleaver. Either bamboo racks or a support placed inside a pot may be used for steaming, a mesh strainer for deep-frying, a spatula for stir-frying, and a ladle for soup. Long chopsticks are handy for beating eggs, mixing sauce ingredients, and handling individual pieces in cooking.

The first step in cooking comes with shopping for ingredients. Following my parents example, I look for produce in season and try to select the freshest vegetables. When vegetables are out of season, I do use frozen peas, green beans, and spinach in preference to canned. Leafy greens like bok choy, flowering mustard, chard, and other members of the *brassica* family have always been the most common vegetables in home-cooking, and provide important nutrients to the diet. In this family, broccoli is a very popular choice. Freshness is particularly important with any seafood, preferably live, but never frozen. It is almost impossible to get fresh-killed poultry, but again frozen should be avoided because flavor and texture are altered.

The preparation of ingredients often takes more time than the actual cooking. After washing, vegetables are cut into uniform pieces for both appearance and to ensure even heating. Cutting, usually with a cleaver, is in dice, shreds, slices, or chunks. Meat cooked with the vegetables should be cut in similar shapes. Meat is usually marinated in soy sauce, wine, and cornstarch to season it and to keep the pieces moist and tender. Seafood may be freshened in salted water.

The specific vegetables or meats are less important to Cantonese dishes than the very distinctive seasonings of the region. Indispensable are the aromatic plants: ginger, garlic, and scallions (green onions). These are necessary to neutralize the stronger flavors of fish and red meats, in addition to enhancing other foods. Ginger, in particular, has healing properties (eases nasal congestion, stimulates appetite, and serves as a tonic), and its "heat" balances the "cold" of crabs and other seafood. Cilantro or Chinese parsley is another strong flavor which some Chinese people enjoy.

Above: Melinda and I stir-frying vegetables in the wok.

In the past, salt was so valuable that it was seldom used in its usual form in cooking. Saltiness came from ingredients which had been preserved in salt or brine. The almost universal soy sauce is a ferment of the soybean and brine. Other soy products made with salt, flour, fruit, wine, or hot peppers provide distinctive regional seasonings. Bean curd preserved in wine and a slightly sweet bean paste are popular in Cantonese cooking. Pickling is another process which preserves seasoned food. Salty seasonings which are distinctively Cantonese include salt fish and shrimp, a fermented black bean and garlic sauce, oyster sauce, and shrimp paste (similar to anchovy paste). They are the flavors Cantonese associate with home-cooking, and an almost endless variety of dishes can be produced with just these seasonings. I am particularly fond of using oyster sauce combined with fragrant sesame oil or black bean and garlic sauce in my own cooking. The former produces a mellow flavor and the latter a robust one.

I never use MSG, a flavor enhancer which was once processed from a variety of seaweed, but is now a chemical product generally used to mask undesirable qualities (i.e., lack of freshness) in food. My mother taught me a simple method to stimulate the taste buds by combining a pinch of sugar with a pinch of salt. The result is neither sweetness nor saltiness, but an intriguing taste sensation which should augment the natural flavors of the fresh vegetables or meat in the dish. This contrast in flavors is the secret of sweet and sour sauce, sour and hot soup, garlic and black bean sauce, and the more complex five spice seasoning. Seasonings from other regions (hot chili combinations and curries) have been transformed by the Cantonese into their own versions. No one spice or seasoning predomi-

nates, nor should the sauce be overwhelming; everything should be balanced. That is the ideal in seasoning, just as the cooking method should achieve the perfect texture.

Meats that have been cooked with little seasoning—plain chicken or pork—or deep fried foods are usually served with a choice of seasonings at the table: dipping sauces of soy, vinegar, mustard, or flavored oils, oyster sauce, seasoned salt and pepper. In a hot pot meal, the diners mix their own flavoring sauce from a variety of condiments. Guests have the opportunity to follow individual preferences, just as the Cantonese cook has occasion to improvise and adapt the recipes of others who have gone before. Unlike the classic French chef, the Chinese pride themselves upon innovation, rather than fidelity to a standard recipe.

Dried ingredients are valued for both texture and seasoning. The dehydrating process, beyond preserving fresh foods, concentrates flavor, and in some instances improves upon the original. The Chinese prefer dried black mushrooms or orange peel to the fresh versions. Dried foods should be soaked to soften before cooking. Besides black mushrooms and orange peel, common dehydrated items on my pantry shelf are wood or cloud ear fungi (crunchy and good for the heart), tiger lily buds, seaweed, shrimp, scallops, oysters, bamboo shoots, lotus seeds, jujubes (Chinese dates), bean curd skin, and noodles (wheat, rice, and mung bean). Other dried products (ginseng, angelica root, dioscorea, astragalus, mangosteen, and wolfberries) are specifically classified as herbal supplements, although everything we eat should contribute to our health.

Father used to quote a saying to the effect that the more we eat of something delicious, the less tasty it becomes. The moral is to avoid greediness and appreciate a delicacy for what it is, for even the greatest gourmet treat palls when eaten to excess. However, it is well within everyone's expectation to eat nourishing food cooked to the proper doneness and seasoned to augment and enhance flavor. Banquets, celebrations, and festivals may bring out more elaborate dishes and special foods, but everyday meals should taste just as good. That is the true spirit of Chinese cooking.

Rice & Noodles

(Fan Mein)

RICE AND NOODLES

My parents, whose ancestors tilled paddy fields in the humid valleys of Guangdong Province for hundreds of years, looked upon rice as the staff of life. Elsewhere in China, in the cooler, drier, wheat-growing regions, steamed bread and noodles are the staples, but my mother continued to look upon rice-based meals as the only ones truly satisfying.

Some of my earliest memories of family meals—reinforced over the years at many other tables—include the familiar sensation of a warm rice bowl in my left hand, the fresh aroma of the just-steamed rice, the anticipation of the taste and texture of each morsel I select from the various dishes, and then each bite with the mouthful of soft rice to clear the mouth before the next. How can this delightful combination ever be boring, or the unfailing perfect base of fluffy rice ever be bland? Just as every meal seemed different, every successive mouthful had its own savor!

My parents, like most Cantonese, preferred long grain rice, which we purchased in large burlap sacks from Texas. I was always told to wash the rice for family meals very carefully in several changes of water to get out all of the talc and grit. The soaking before cooking helped to soften the rice, which should be in fluffy, tender, separate grains when cooked. Rice comes in many varieties, and some people prefer the shorter grain, which cooks into a stickier rice. The very special variety known as glutinous, or sweet, rice is a high-vitamin, more expensive (lower yield per acre), round grain that cooks into a very sticky rice that is often used in making holiday dishes. I associate its chewy and "stick-to-the-ribs" texture with many festive foods: leaf-wrapped dumplings for the Dragon Boat Festival, Chinese New Year's puddings, and sweet dumplings in soup at my wedding.

As rice must not be wasted, my mother had ways to use up any that was left over—from pots of gruel for breakfast to fried rice with bits of vegetables and meat for flavoring. A small amount can be reheated by placing it over the freshly cooked rice just before the pot is covered for the final cooking. This dual use of one pot is also the technique my mother used to heat up dried Chinese sausages. As the sausage plumps on top of the rice, it adds a delectable flavor to the whole pot. The sausage is then sliced up as a side dish for the meal. A variation of this method is used in making one dish rice casseroles—a quick and easy answer to the question of what to cook for one or two people. I think of these all-in-one meals as a miniature version of the usual rice-plus-dishes lunch.

Noodle dishes are a form of Chinese fast food. The busy worker in Chinese communities drops into noodle shops or street stands for a quick bowl of noodles in broth or a dish of chow mein—stir-fried noodles. My mother may have looked upon these as mere snacks, but I have learned to enjoy all kinds of noodles, whether as a satisfying one-dish lunch or as a fun way to entertain a crowd at an informal party. Noodles are available either fresh or dried, in shapes from angel hair to wide, and in rice stick form or wheat flour based. The narrower shapes absorb the sauce more, and the wider forms don't break up when stir-fried.

Above: Commercially available packaged noodles.

BAK FAN
BASIC WHITE RICE

My mother always stressed the importance of cooking the rice just right for each meal. That meant I had to take great care in washing the raw rice and in measuring out the correct amount of water. I no longer rinse the rice so many times and I now use measuring cups instead of the old rule-of-thumb. For a large group, I even use a rice cooker. Although my mother did not consider brown rice worthy of her meals, I use it sometimes for its nutritional value. Soaking the rice for an hour or more before cooking does make it softer.

2 cups long grain rice
3 cups water

A pot with a tightly fitting lid is best for cooking rice. Bring the rice and water to a boil in an uncovered pot. Give the rice a quick stir as it boils. When most of the surface water begins to be absorbed, cover the pot, and lower the heat to the lowest setting. Leave the pot to simmer untouched for 15 or 20 minutes. Turn off the heat. The rice will remain hot until ready to serve. Fluff the rice before placing in serving container.

Short grain rice is cooked with less water, and greater quantities of rice require less than the ratio of 1 and 1/2 cups of water to one of rice. A shorter grain or more water will result in a sticker rice—what my mother called "broke" rice.

Serves 3 to 4.

JUK
RICE GRUEL (CONGEE)

This traditional breakfast cereal was probably invented as a way of using up leftover rice from the evening meal. Water would be added to the pot and left to cook slowly in the lingering heat of the stove, to be reheated in the morning by a rekindled fire. Hot bowls of the juk would be eaten with leftover tidbits, pickles, or salted preserves. It is easily digested, perfect for baby food and soothing fare for invalids.

1 cup cooked rice
4 cups water

Add water to the rice and bring to boil. After a few minutes, turn down the heat to simmer for about two hours or more. Stir occasionally. The rice should be completely broken up in the thickened gruel. I like to eat it by pouring the juk into a bowl with some leftover meat and vegetables, reheating them in the process. Then a bit of seasoning—soy sauce, oyster sauce, or chopped green onions—make a quick meal.

Serves 2 to 3.

Right: This is an early picture of me with my mother in our backyard in Canonsburg.

YEANG JIEU CHAU FAN
COLORFUL FRIED RICE

This is a creative way to use leftover rice, meat and vegetables, but it is such a favorite that it's worth making from scratch for a festive buffet. The ingredients may vary according to what's available, but there should be a variety of colors and textures.

(Illustrated opposite)

2 cups cooked rice (any just cooked
    should be allowed to cool)
1 or 2 eggs, well stirred
3 tablespoons oil, though less is needed
    with a non-stick pan
1/2 teaspoon minced ginger root
1 small white onion chopped
2 scallions sliced diagonally
1/4 pound fresh mushrooms, sliced
1 small red sweet pepper, sliced
1/2 cup peas, thawed if frozen
1/2 cup diced leftover meat or ham
(Mother used barbecued pork)

SEASONING SAUCE:
1/4 cup chicken broth
dash of salt and pepper
1 teaspoon oyster sauce
1/2 teaspoon sesame oil

Mix seasoning sauce. Have all ingredients prepared before heating the wok. Swirl a tablespoon of the oil into the wok and pour in the eggs. As they set, use the spatula to break the eggs into pieces before removing from the pan.

Add another tablespoon of the oil and add the vegetables in the following order: ginger, onions, peppers, mushrooms, and peas. When they are thoroughly heated, add the scallions and the last of the oil, drizzling it down the side of the wok. Stir in the rice and the reserved egg. As the rice heats pour in the seasoning sauce and mix all ingredients until the sauce is thorough absorbed. If necessary, cover briefly to make sure the rice is hot.

Serves 4 to 6 when part of a meal.

FOH GAI JUK
TURKEY RICE GRUEL

The Cantonese are fond of more elaborate versions of juk, which feature poultry, pork, or fish added to the cooking pot. The added ingredients plus the broth produces a full-bodied dish, which will feed a crowd at an informal party with little fuss or expense! During the winter, mixing in glutinous rice increases the nutritional benefits of a heartier one-pot meal. The following recipe is also a good way to feed a houseful of holiday guests!

1 turkey carcass, or a whole chicken
3 quarts of water
several slices of ginger
1/2 teaspoon salt
2 cups uncooked rice, one of which can
    be glutinous
1/2 cup nut meats (peanuts, chestnuts, or
    cashews)
1/2 cup diced carrots or other root
    vegetable

Place the turkey carcass or chicken in a pot with the water, salt and ginger. Cook for an hour or two until a rich broth is produced. Strain the broth, and discard the bones. Chicken meat may be kept to add to the juk, or seasoned and served with it. Add the washed uncooked rice to the broth and cook for two or more hours, adding the nut meats and vegetables about mid-way through. Stir occasionally to prevent burning on the bottom.

Serve the juk in individual bowls, with each guest helping himself from dishes of seasonings and condiments: sesame oil, soy sauce, oyster sauce, chili oil, shredded scallions, parsley (cilantro), shredded ham.

Serves 10 to 12.

LOTUS LEAF WRAPPED RICE

In this Cantonese specialty, not only does the lotus leaf impart a delectable fragrance to the bundled rice mixture, but the Chinese believe that the essence of the leaves provides all manner of health benefits to the diner. Fresh leaves are not generally available here, but dried ones can be substituted. The rice can be steamed in one large bundle or, if the leaves are small, divided into two or more bundles with the steaming time reduced. This makes an elegant way to serve rice in a guest meal.

(Illustrated opposite)

2 or more lotus leaves, soaked to soften
3/4 cup long grain rice
3/4 cup glutinous rice
2 cups water
2 links Chinese sausage, steamed
1/4 pound roast pork, diced
1/4 cup dried shrimp, softened (or substitute 1/2 cup fresh small shrimp)
1/4 pound cooked chicken or duck, diced
5 dried mushrooms, diced
1/3 cup bamboo shoots, diced
1/2 cup cooked lotus seeds (or roasted unsalted cashews)
1 slice ginger, minced
1 scallion, chopped
2 tablespoons cooking oil
1 tablespoon rice wine
1 tablespoon soy sauce
1 tablespoon oyster sauce
1 teaspoon sugar
1 teaspoon salt
1/4 teaspoon pepper
1 teaspoon sesame oil
Twine to tie the wrapping

Wash, soak and cook the two kinds of rice in the water. After the rice as cooked over low heat for about ten minutes, the sausage can be placed on top and covered tightly again to continue cooking for ten more minutes. Allow the rice to cool to room temperature and dice the sausage.

Heat the cooking oil in a wok and stir fry the ginger, scallions, mushrooms, bamboo and dried shrimp. Remove and combine with the diced pork, chicken, lotus seeds and all of the seasonings except the sesame oil. Now mix together with the rice.

Dry the soaked leaves, remove any tough stems if they prevent the leaf from folding easily, and overlap two leaves if necessary to form the wrapping. If you are making more than one bundle, divide the leaves accordingly. Brush the inside of the leaves with the sesame oil and place the rice mixture in the middle. Wrap the leaves around the rice to form a square bundle. Tie with twine.

Place the bundle or bundles on a rack over steam and cook for half an hour if a single bundle, or for 20 minutes if two. The contents should be heated through. Untie the bundle at the table to serve hot.

Serves 8 or more.

Below: Three siblings of two generations: Fifth uncle, eldest uncle and father, with Ethel, Tom and I in about 1938.

BEEF FRIED RICE

This hearty lunch dish can be assembled with leftovers. As part of a family meal, a small amount of chopped meat goes a long way.

1/2 pound chopped beef
3 cups cooked rice
1 cup peas, parboiled
1 teaspoon minced ginger
2 scallions, chopped
1 clove garlic, minced (optional)
1 tablespoon soy sauce
1 teaspoon sugar
1/2 teaspoon salt and pepper
2 tablespoons cooking oil

Heat the oil in the wok and add the scallions, ginger and garlic, along with the chopped beef. Cook until beef changes color. Add the soy sauce, salt, sugar and pepper and stir. Next add the rice and peas and mix well with the the contents of the wok to blend seasonings. Serve hot.

Serves 4 or more.

LONG LIFE NOODLES

Traditionally, birthdays are celebrations of great age and not parties for children. Sixty, the multiple of the cycle of twelve horoscope animals used to designate years and the five elements, is considered a full life span. As years increase beyond 60 to 70 or 80, there is even more reason for felicitations and special banquets.

Extra long noodles have come to symbolize longevity and noodle dishes are usually served at birthday celebrations. Here is a festive version of noodles in a rich broth combined with choice ingredients. Care must be taken to avoid breaking the noodles as one cooks or eats.

1 pound long egg noodles, preferably fresh
1/2 pound chicken breast, thinly sliced
1/2 pound fresh shrimp, shelled and veined
1/4 pound fresh mushrooms, sliced
1/4 pound snow peas
1/2 cup sliced bamboo shoots or fresh lotus root
4 dried mushrooms, softened and sliced
2 scallions, sliced
2 slices ginger root, mashed
6 cups rich chicken broth
1 tablespoon soy sauce
1 teaspoon sugar
1/2 teaspoon salt
dash of pepper
1/2 teaspoon sesame oil
1 slice ham, slivered (optional) for garnish

MARINADE:
1 egg white
1 tablespoon rice wine
1/2 teaspoon salt
1 tablespoon cornstarch

Place the prepared chicken slices and the shrimp in separate bowls. Mix the marinade and place half in each bowl. Stir and set aside for about half an hour. Meanwhile, cook the noodles in boiling water, about 3-5 minutes for fresh and twice as long for dried. Rinse and drain well.

Set the chicken broth to heat in a large pot. In another pot, heat water to a simmer and briefly cook the marinated chicken slices and shrimp until the color changes but the pieces are not completely cooked through. Drain well.

When the broth boils, add the ginger, scallions, and vegetables. Return to a boil, and then add the chicken, shrimp, and noodles. Next, the seasonings are stirred in to blend. Correct according to taste, and pour into a soup tureen to serve with the ham slivers sprinkled on top.

As part of a special dinner, this will serve 6 to 8.

ZHA JIANG MEIN
NOODLES WITH SPICY MEAT SAUCE

The spiciness of this dish, which originated in Sichuan, can be adjusted according to your taste by altering the amount of hot pepper in the seasoning. It is a family favorite, which is easily prepared for larger crowds.

green pepper, six green onions, and a cucumber

1/2 pound thin egg noodles, cooked in boiling water for about 3 minutes, drained and tossed with a small amount of sesame oil.

MEAT SAUCE INGREDIENTS:

1/3 pound ground meat (pork, chicken, or veal)

1 tablespoon minced ginger root

2 scallions, chopped

2 cloves of garlic, minced

1/4 teaspoon or more red pepper flakes

1/4 cup ground bean sauce

1 teaspoon sugar

1/4 cup broth

Chop the green pepper, six green onions, and cucumber. Place in separate bowls and set aside. Heat a wok, add a tablespoon of cooking oil and cook the ginger, the 2 scallions, garlic and pepper flakes to release flavors. Add the ground meat and stir until the meat loses color. Add the ground bean sauce and sugar and mix well before pouring in the broth. Simmer for about 15 minutes or until most of the broth has been absorbed, stirring several times.

Serve the sauce over the noodles, adding the garnishes to mix and add texture.

Serves 4 or more as part of a meal.

JIHT MAH MEIN
SESAME NOODLES

Here is another easy noodle dish in which the accompanying ingredients can vary from meat and vegetables to all vegetables, depending upon what you have handy.

1/2 pound egg noodles

1/4 pound pork, cut in strips

MARINADE:

2 teaspoons soy sauce

1 teaspoon wine

2 teaspoons cornstarch

2 scallions, sliced diagonally

1 clove garlic, crushed

1 carrot shredded

2 tablespoons cooking oil

SAUCE:

2 tablespoons sesame paste, or peanut butter

1 tablespoon soy sauce

1 tablespoon wine

1 teaspoon salt

1 teaspoon sugar

2 teaspoons sesame oil

1/2 cup chicken broth

Marinate the pork in the soy, wine, and cornstarch mixture and set aside for half an hour. Prepare the noodles by boiling until just done. Drain.

Heat the oil in the wok and add the garlic. The clove can be removed or left in before adding the marinated pork to stir-fry. Remove the pork and reserve.

Add the scallions and carrots and stir for several minutes to cook. Then return the pork with the sauce ingredients. Stir and add the drained noodles to blend and heat through. Serve hot.

Serves 3 or 4.

NOODLES STIR-FRIED WITH BARBECUED PORK

Noodle dishes are a natural quick lunch. They can be made into soup noodles or dishes topped with some savory accompaniment. Leftover meats and handy vegetables can be quickly stir-fried together with some sauce to serve as a topping. Here is a popular Cantonese version of such a lunch platter.

(Illustrated opposite)

1/2 pound egg noodles
1/4 pound barbecued pork (or ham or
    Chinese sausage),sliced
2 stalks of Chinese cabbage (or spinach
    or chard), cut in bite-sized pieces
1 small zucchini, halved and sliced
3 dried mushrooms, softened and sliced
1 sliced ginger root, crushed
1 clove garlic, crushed
1 scallion, sliced
2 tablespoons cooking oil

SAUCE:
1 tablespoon soy sauce
1 tablespoon oyster sauce
1 teaspoon sugar
1/2 teaspoon salt
1/4 teaspoon pepper
1 tablespoon rice wine
1/4 cup chicken broth

Prepare the noodles by boiling until just done, and drain.

Heat the oil and stir in the ginger and garlic until the flavor is released. Then remove. Add the cabbage, zucchini, mushrooms, and scallions to the oil and stir until just about done. Add the barbecued pork and the sauce and stir to mix. Finally, add the noodles and mix thoroughly to heat through and absorb the sauce. Serve hot.

Serves 3 to 4.

SIZZLING RICE CRUST

Here is another inventive way to use leftover rice. When rice is kept too long over a low flame, a crust forms from the rice on the bottom and sides of the pot. Mother used to add some water to this crust and let it cook while we ate. It was softened enough for a second helping of rice to consist of this toasty-tasting chewy rice. I was very fond of it and never worried about leaving the rice a bit longer over the fire. This occurred often enough in rice cooking that popular dishes were developed to make use of this crust.

Allow the crust to dry thoroughly. Break into pieces a few inches in size and deep fry the pieces in oil just hot enough to turn the crust golden, but not deep brown.

These crusts serve as the base for Sizzling Rice Soups (see pages 32 and 56). The crusts must be deep-fried just before the dish is served, kept hot in a heated platter or dish. Prepared crusts can be frozen for later use.

Below: Mother and granddaughters at Golden Gate Park in 1970. Cathy, Melinda and Tania called mother "Po Po."

SAVORY WRAPPED RICE DUMPLINGS

Leaf-wrapped, glutinous rice dumplings are seasonal delicacies made during the Dragon Boat Festival, which commemorates poet/statesman Qu Yuan (3rd century B.C.) who committed suicide after being exiled by the ruler who failed to heed his sage counsel. These rice offerings were rushed by boatmen to prevent the fish from disturbing the body of their patriotic hero. There are regional variations in the fillings of these dumplings (some are sweet), but Mother always had the most delicious ingredients in hers: The richness of nuts combine with the savory pork, sausage, and salty egg yolks in each mouthful of chewy rice. Either lotus or bamboo leaves may be used to wrap the djong. Making these dumplings is a fun activity for family and friends.

(Illustrated opposite)

3 cups uncooked glutinous rice, soaked overnight and drained

1 cup roasted chestnuts, cashews, or lotus seeds

3 links Chinese sausage, steamed to soften and sliced

1/3 pound barbecued pork, diced

2 salted egg yolks, cut up (optional)

2 tablespoons soy sauce

1 teaspoon sugar

1/2 teaspoon salt

12 bamboo or lotus leaves, soaked to soften

string to tie the wrapping

Below: Ethel, Tom and I in Canonsburg.

Combine the rice with all of the other ingredients and seasonings. Take a leaf and form a cone shape at one end. Hold this in your left hand and carefully fill the hollow with the rice mixture. Do not pack, as you must allow room within the wrapping for expansion of the rice during cooking.

Wrap the leaf over the filling, overlapping to shape a plump tricorn. None of the filling must show. Use the string to tie the dumpling wrapping around the middle and to keep the leaf from opening during cooking.

Place the wrapped dumplings in a pot, cover with water and simmer for two hours or until done. Unwrap to eat warm. They may be reheated by reboiling or by steaming (unwrapped).

Serves 12.

SINGAPORE RICE NOODLES

The Chinese who emigrated to Malaysia adopted local spices into their cooking, and the resulting dishes have become popular throughout the overseas Chinese communities. Noodle menus from San Francisco to Hong Kong and London feature some version of this curry-flavored combination of seafood, vegetables and rice noodles. This rice product, more common to the southern regions of China, has a different texture from the northern wheat noodles and cooks more rapidly. Overcooking makes the noodles mushy.

(Illustrated opposite)

1/2 pound rice noodles (sometimes called "rice sticks")
1/3 pound shrimps (other seafood-squid, crab, etc.- may be included), sliced.
1/2 cup sliced bamboo shoots or water chestnuts
1/2 cup sliced cooked meat (chicken, barbequed pork, ham, etc.)
1 small onion, sliced in segments
2 slices ginger root, shredded
2 teaspoons or more curry paste
1 tablespoon soy sauce
2 teaspoons sugar
1 teaspoon salt
1/2 cup broth
2 tablespoons cooking oil

Soak the noodles in hot water for 10 or 15 minutes until soft. If you are using wide noodles, parboil for a minute or two. Drain thoroughly and set aside.

Prepare the meat, shrimp, and vegetables. Heat half the oil in the wok and stir-fry the shrimp until they change color, being careful not to overcook. Remove from the wok and set aside.

Add the rest of the oil and stir in the onion and ginger. Add the bamboo shoots, curry paste, and the meat slices, stirring well to mix. Soy sauce, sugar, salt, and broth are added next and heated. Then, the shrimp and noodles are combined with the contents of the wok until the broth and seasonings are absorbed. Serve immediately.

Serves 4.

SOUP NOODLES WITH TOPPING

Here is a simple way to prepare a lunch using noodles, broth, and left-over meat and vegetables which is lower-fat than pan-fried noodle dishes. This is a very popular lunch with Chinese people everywhere.

2 ounces of noodles per person
1 and 1/2 cup broth per person

ASSORTED TOPPINGS:
cooked meats—barbecued pork, ham, chicken, beef, seafood
blanched vegetables—snow peas, peas, cabbage, mushrooms, etc.
eggs, chopped scallions, cilantro

SEASONINGS:
soy sauce
oyster sauce
chili oil
salt and pepper
sesame oil

Have the noodles cooked and drained while the broth is being heated. Place some of the desired seasonings and the noodles in each bowl. Next, add a selection of the toppings, and then pour the broth over everything.

Stir to mix the seasonings, and enjoy.

SOUPS
(GENG)

SOUPS

When I was growing up, family meals always included a *geng,* or soup. After finishing my bowl of rice—or to help the last grains get down — I filled the bowl with soup. This was what I drank at meals instead of water or milk. Mother's soups were as varied as the other dishes she cooked. I remember clear summer soups which were supposed to produce a "cooling" effect, and hearty winter broths full of "warming" ingredients. Even more important for family health were the specifically herbal concoctions which were good for "clearing out the system" or "fending off bronchial congestion." Whatever the purpose of the ever-changing soups, I thought they were delicious!

Mother's soup-making demonstrated her ability to get the most out of her ingredients. With a few pork chops on hand, she would first slice the meat for a steamed or stir-fry dish; the bones would be boiled in some water for a quick soup base. She did the same with chicken bones and giblets. A richer broth is made from cooking bones for several hours. In making one's own broth, the amount of salt can be kept within limits—unlike using canned soups. The classic Chinese broth is made with little or no salt, but with ginger and scallions. Besides its use as a soup base, chicken broth is also an important ingredient in sauces for other dishes. Some should always be kept on hand. If canned broth is used, look for the lower salt kind or reduce the seasoning in the dish.

The light soups are usually cooked in 15 minutes; the heavy soups are long-simmered and make use of many dehydrated and preserved ingredients.

The light soups make best use of fresh vegetables in season, whereas the heavier broths tide the family over the winter months. Among the slow-simmered soups are the elegant banquet dishes of shark's fin soup, bird's nest soup, and soup made in a whole winter melon—all of which my father produced at very special meals for the family. Far from being a preliminary course, soups are often the highlight of a Chinese meal.

Above: Here I am in the kitchen with my soup pot.

MUSTARD GREEN SOUP

This is another "cooling" soup, a variation upon many tonic spring broths. The slight bitterness of the mustard green is much appreciated as a distinct flavor by the Cantonese. Besides its use in this soup, this vegetable is usually preserved and used in winter soups.

1 bunch mustard greens, cut into bite-sized segments

1 quart broth

2 slices ginger root

1/4 cup dried shrimp, soaked and rinsed (or shredded ham)

pinches of salt, sugar, and pepper

Place all of the ingredients into a pot and bring to a boil. Simmer for 15 minutes. A few drops of cooked or sesame oil may be added before serving.

Serves 4 or 5.

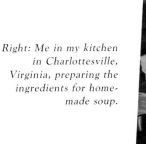

Right: Me in my kitchen in Charlottesville, Virginia, preparing the ingredients for home-made soup.

BEAN CURD SOUP WITH VEGETABLES

This satisfying summer soup uses fresh garden vegetables. Make it colorful, as well as nutritious, by using tomatoes with dark, leafy greens—chard, Chinese cabbage, or spinach.

1 pound bean curd, cut into 3/4-inch cubes

1 large tomato, peeled and deseeded, and cut into segments

3 cups tender leafy greens, cut in half-inch slices

6 fresh mushrooms, sliced

1 teaspoon shredded ginger root

1 scallion, chopped

1 clove crushed garlic

l quart broth

1 tablespoon soy sauce

1 teaspoon sugar

1 teaspoon salt

dash of pepper or hot pepper oil

1 teaspoon sesame oil

Prepare all the ingredients in a pot and bring to a boil. Simmer for 10 to 12 minutes. The addition of a handful of noodles would make this a one-dish meal.

Serves 4 to 6.

WATERCRESS SOUP

This is one of my favorite summer soups from Mother's wide repertoire. I can still recall the refreshing taste of this clear light broth on a sunny day.

(Illustrated opposite)

1 bunch watercress, well washed and cut
    into sections
1 quart chicken or vegetable broth
1 slice ginger root
pinch of pepper
pinch of salt
a few drops of sesame oil

Mother used her pork bones base for this soup, but chicken broth is just as good. Start the broth to boil with the ginger, Add the watercress, the salt and pepper. Cook for about 10 minutes.

The watercress should still be fresh and green. The addition of a few drops of sesame oil be fore serving enhances the delicate taste of the watercress. This is considered a "cooling" soup.

Serves 4 to 5.

Above: Melinda and I choosing fresh ginger root to make Watercress Soup.

TOMATO EGG FLOWER SOUP

Here is another of Mother's quick soups, a favorite during the height of the tomato season.

(Illustrated opposite)

1 large or 2 medium tomatoes, cut into wedges
1 quart broth
1 egg lightly stirred
2 scallions sliced diagonally in 2-inch segments
pinch of salt, sugar, and pepper

Bring broth to a boil and add all of the ingredients except the egg. Simmer for 10 minutes. Stir in the egg to form "flowers" in the soup just before serving.

Serves 4 or 5.

CORN AND CHICKEN SOUP

Creamed corn soup, once the result of processing fresh corn, is now quite easy to prepare using the modern convenience of canned cream-style corn. However, if you are willing to make this from scratch with ears of fresh corn, you can remove the kernels, mash them, and use them instead. This elegant version uses light velvet chicken (see page 104) with the corn. Other equally delicious variations can be made with crabmeat or minced ham.

1 chicken breast, minced
1 tablespoon wine
1/2 teaspoon salt
1 egg white
5 cups chicken broth
1 can cream-style corn
dash of sugar and pepper
1/4 teaspoon sesame oil
1/8 pound of ham, minced (optional)

Mince the chicken breast and mix in the wine, salt and egg white.

Heat the chicken broth and, as it simmers, add the chicken mixture and stir to keep the pieces small as they poach. Add the can of creamed corn and, as the soup thoroughly heats, add the rest of the seasonings.

The minced ham can be added to the top of each bowl of soup as it is served.

Serves 4 to 6.

Above: This is a picture of Tom, me and Ethel when we were very young.

DRIED OYSTER, DRIED BOK CHOY, AND DRIED TOFU SOUP

This Cantonese mainstay, never found on restaurant menus, is my personal favorite of my mother's winter broths. For this dish, I willingly peeled water chestnuts (eating a few as my reward), and the smells of the soup simmering is associated in my mind with cold weather. All of the dried ingredients should be soaked overnight, or for several hours, to soften. The oysters should be carefully cleaned of any sand.

(Illustrated opposite)

1 quart broth

6 dried oysters

2 sheets dried tofu skin (fu juk)

1/2 pound fresh water chestnuts, peeled (canned may be substituted)

6 dried Chinese red dates (jujubes)

6 slices of dried Chinese yam

a pinch of salt if necessary after tasting

Place ingredients in pot to boil. Skim, and simmer for at least an hour before serving. Check for seasoning, adding a bit of salt if necessary.

Serves 4 to 5.

FRESH OYSTER AND LETTUCE SOUP

This soup was a special treat in Pennsylvania, where fresh oysters were a rare delicacy. In my parents' native region, oysters were so common that oyster sauce became a major flavoring.

1/4 pound of Napa cabbage, cut into bite-sized pieces

1/4 pound of fresh oysters, well washed

1 quart broth

2 slices ginger root

1/4 pound of fresh mushrooms, sliced

pinch of salt and pepper

Place the ingredients into a pot and bring to a boil. Simmer for 15 minutes. Check and correct the seasonings.

Serves 4 to 5.

Right: Here I am choosing the dried oysters to make Dried Oyster, Dried Bok Choy and Dried Tofu Soup.

WON TON SOUP

This soup, chock-full with filled dumplings, counts as a complete lunch. I like to fill the won ton myself in order to make them plump with lots of shrimp.

The broth should be a rich, home-made chicken broth, and the other ingredients can vary with the vegetables in season, preferably a leafy green type.

(Illustrated opposite)

one packet of won ton skins,
   about 3 dozen.
3/4 pound shrimp, chopped coarsely
1/2 pound ground meat (veal, pork, etc.)
2 tablespoons minced scallions
1 tablespoon minced ginger
2 tablespoons chopped water chestnuts
   or bamboo shoots
1 tablespoon wine or dry sherry
1 teaspoon chili oil
1 tablespoon soy sauce
1 teaspoon cornstarch
dash of salt and sugar
6 cups chicken broth
1/4 pound of bok choy, Napa cabbage or
   other leafy green vegetable, sliced
1 tablespoon cornstarch dissolved in a
   tablespoon of water

Mix the filling by combining the shrimp, ground meat, scallions, ginger, water chestnuts, wine, oil, soy sauce, one teaspoon of cornstarch, salt and sugar.

Make the dumplings by placing a heaping teaspoon or so of the filling on each three-inch wrapper. The dumplings can be sealed in several ways by using the cornstarch mixture. My method is to bring two opposite corners together, but not quite overlapping. Seal the triangular edges together. Then the two side points can be brought together and sealed to form a cap shape.

These dumplings can be deep fried as an appetizer, but I much prefer them in soup. Bring a pot of water to a boil and add a batch of the won ton. When they float to the surface, add a cup of cold water and allow the water to come to a boil again. This ensures thorough cooking of the filling.

Meanwhile, the chicken broth can be heated in another pot with the greens added to cook.

The usual way of serving won ton soup is to place about six of the dumplings in each bowl and pour some of the broth into each before serving each guest. Correct seasonings according to taste. Some people like to add some sesame or soy sauce to the broth, along with some chopped green scallions.

Serves 6 or more as part of a multi-course meal.

Above: Here are Melinda and shopping for vegetables. You can use any type of leafy green vegetable in your Won Tons.

SOUR AND HOT SOUP

When Mother used to dress fresh chickens, the smooth, congealed blood was used in a rich soup. This ingredient was often used in the very popular sour and hot soup, a spicy melange of flavors and textures which has many regional variations. Since I never have occasion to work with live chickens, this recipe uses bean curd instead. If you wish a totally vegetarian version, omit the meat as well. The degree of spiciness can be adjusted by increasing the amount of hot oil.

1 quart chicken or vegetable stock
1/2 pound firm bean curd, cut into strips
1/2 pound cooked pork or other meat, cut into strips
5 dried mushrooms, softened and cut into strips
1/3 cup bamboo shoots, shredded
1/3 cup dried lily buds (gim jim), softened and hard tips removed
2 tablespoons dried wood ears fungi (muk ngih), softened and rinsed
1 slice ginger root, shredded
1 scallion, shredded
1 egg, beaten
1 tablespoon rice wine
1 tablespoon soy sauce
2 tablespoons rice vinegar
1/2 teaspoon salt
1/2 teaspoon pepper
1/2 teaspoon or more hot pepper oil
1/2 teaspoon sesame oil
2 teaspoons cornstarch mixed with 1 tablespoon broth or water

Heat the stock to a boil in a pot and add the shredded mushrooms, bamboo shoots, lily buds, wood ears, and ginger.

Return the soup to not quite boiling and add the bean curd, pork, scallion, and the seasonings—wine, soy sauce, vinegar, salt, pepper and hot oil.

Stir in the beaten egg slowly to form flowery strands. Thicken with the cornstarch mixture before serving hot.

Serves 4 or more.

DUCK SOUP

Here is the easy answer to the question: What to do with the carcass from a roast duck? Nothing simpler than to make it into this tasty duck broth, into which a few vegetables are added to create a soup fit for imperial tastes. Moreover, the broth can also serve as the base for a distinctive rice gruel. The vegetables should complement the richness of the duck soup.

1 carcass from a roast duck
2 slices ginger root
3 scallions, sliced in 3-inch pieces
10 cups water
2 cups sliced vegetables (celery cabbage, chard, or other leafy greens)
sliced fresh mushrooms
shredded white giant radish, or cubes of bean curd.
1 teaspoon sugar
1/2 teaspoon salt, or to taste
dash of pepper

Place the carcass in a large pot with 10 cups of water. Add the ginger and scallions and bring to a boil. Skim and reduce heat to simmer for about two hours. Strain the broth, cool and remove fat.
Prepare soup by heating the broth and adding the vegetables and seasonings. Simmer for 10 to 15 minutes, correct seasonings and serve hot.

Serves 6 or more as part of a meal.

(Illustrated above)

GAI DIU
NEW MOTHER'S CHICKEN SOUP

This rich soup laced with wine is the formula for building up a new mother's strength after childbirth. Traditionally, a mother-in-law prepares it for her daughter-in-law in recognition of her producing a grandchild. When my older daughter Melinda was born, this was the recipe my family urged my husband to make for me.

1 whole chicken, with giblets

1 quart of water

1/4 cup wood ears fungi

3 slices of ginger root

6 dried mushrooms, soaked to soften

6 red dates

1/4 cup lotus seeds

1/4 cup dried lily buds (golden needles), soaked to soften

1/3 cup rice wine or sherry

Place all ingredients except the wine into a pot and bring to a boil. Skim well. Simmer for about an hour. Just before serving, pour in the wine. Pieces of the chicken can be eaten with the soup. Some recipes call for stronger spirits.

Serves 4 or more.

(Illustrated above)

WHOLE WINTER MELON SOUP

This rich soup cooked in a whole winter melon is one of my father's specialties. This dish can be made without the shell, with just pieces of winter melon, but the presentation of this spectacular centerpiece to a feast is well worth the extra time and effort. The more elegant the mixture of ingredients, the richer the flavor of the soup; select a variety of meats and vegetables for balance in color and texture. I have here the combination which I recall my father using for his soup made for a guest meal during the 1940s.

(Illustrated opposite)

1 whole winter melon, about 10 to 12 pounds
1 quart rich chicken broth
1/4 pound chicken breast, velveted (see page 104 in the Poultry section)
1/4 pound shrimp or crabmeat
1/8 pound ham diced
1/4 pound mushrooms, diced
1/4 cup lotus seeds
1/4 pound water chestnuts, diced
2 slices ginger root, minced
1 tablespoon dried shrimp, soaked to soften
a dash of salt, pepper, and sugar
1/2 teaspoon sesame oil

Below: The winter melon after cutting off the top, and before scooping out the seeds.

Cut the top off the winter melon and scoop out the seeds and stringy pulp. If the melon is thick, remove some of it to leave an inch-and-a-half layer inside the rind. Place the melon in a heat-proof dish; tie twine around the melon and dish so that both can be lifted from the steam pot. Place melon and dish on a rack in a steam pot large enough to contain the entire melon when lid is on. Steam the melon for about 45 minutes. (This will shorten the total cooking time.)

Meanwhile, in another pot start the chicken broth cooking with all of the other ingredients except the chicken and shrimp and sesame oil. Pour the soup into the melon after the first steaming. Do not fill the melon to the top; allow about two inches. Add hot water to the steam pot as needed to keep it from running dry. Continue steaming for another hour and a half. Check to see if the melon pulp has turned soft and translucent.

Add the velveted chicken and shrimp or crabmeat and steam for another 10 minutes. Correct seasonings and add sesame oil. Lift out the melon and dish and serve to general applause. Scoop out some of the melon pulp with each serving. The "cool" smoothness of the melon is a delightful complement to the textures of the other ingredients and takes on the rich flavor of the broth.

Serves 6 to 8.

AI BIN LOU
CANTONESE FIRE POT

The charcoal-fired cooking utensil known as Mongolian fire pot (huo guo) which is used to cook lamb strips and cabbage in northern China has been adapted by the Cantonese to include a far richer assortment of meats and vegetables. The wonderful advantage of this guest meal is that everyone does his own cooking. All the host has to do is slice up the raw ingredients and set out sauce makings. The fun of group participation makes for a very convivial dinner—much like the fondue parties of some years ago. If you do not have a copper or brass fire pot, an electric fry pan can be substituted. If you use a charcoal-heated fire pot, be sure that there is adequate ventilation. The meats offered can be any assortment, so long as the pieces are cut so that quick cooking can be done. Some meals can be all-vegetarian or all-seafood. For the host who wants the guests to exert as little effort as possible, an assortment of foods can be placed into the pot in a pretty pattern and the entire dish presented already cooked at the table. All that is required is for the selections to be taken out individually and seasoned by each diner.

This is the sort of fire pot meal I have often served to guests using a copper fire pot purchased decades ago. The hardest task is slicing the meat very thin, more easily done if the meat is first partially frozen and the cleaver well sharpened. All of the ingredients can be prepared and set out artistically on platters ahead of time, and the table set with an array of condiments for each guest to mix according to individual taste. At each place setting is a pair of chopsticks and a long-handled wire basket which will hold the food being cooked in the simmering broth of the pot. Each guest has a plate and a bowl in which he mixes his seasoning sauce, and a spoon for the final soup.

(Illustrated opposite)

1 pound each of very thinly sliced meat: chicken breast, beef, pork tenderloin.
1/2 to 1 pound of shrimp, scallops, or oysters (cut shrimp or scallops if large)
1/2 pound each of noodles, either cellophane or angel hair. (Soften and cut into manageable lengths.)
1/2 pound of mushrooms, sliced
1/2 pound of water chestnuts or sliced jicama
1/2 pound Napa cabbage, in half-inch slices
bean sprouts or snow peas, if fresh (optional)

CONDIMENTS IN BOWLS:
rice wine or dry sherry
soy sauce
sugar
sesame butter
vinegar
sesame oil
chili oil or paste
oyster sauce
round Sichuan pepper
ginger juice
minced garlic
chopped scallions.

Use enough hot broth or water to fill the pot but not too full., so that it won't spill over when the water bubbles or when food is put in to cook. Keep more broth heated to replenish the pot if the liquid boils away and the level is too low. Array condiments in bowls or small pitchers.

If a seasoning mixture is too strong, a bit of the broth will thin it; if too spicy, vinegar will neutralize the zing. I like to start with a combination of wine, soy sauce, sugar, sesame, oyster sauce, ginger, and a small amount of chili—sticking close to my Cantonese roots!

The procedure is to first mix our sauces, then each person can select from the array of ingredients and cooks his own by placing it in the individual long-handled baskets. The traditional way is for each to hold the piece of food in the broth with his chopsticks, but the problem of keeping cooking and eating chopsticks separate is avoided by the baskets. Care should be taken not to overcook the meat, for that toughens it.

Vegetables can be left in the cook longer. At the end, more ingredients are added to the pot if they are still on the platters, the pot covered, and the resultant rich soup is then served as a finale. Seasoning the soup is also an individual matter, using one's leftover sauce.

The appropriate wine to drink with this cold-weather meal is heated rice wine. Saki is a good substitute. The bottle can be kept warm in a pot of simmering water.

Serves 8 to 10. Use a round table so that everyone can reach the central hotpot.

SEAFOOD SIZZLING RICE SOUP

The rice crusts in this showpiece dish may be from leftover rice, but the crusts must be dried by baking in the oven before final crisping by deep frying, then kept hot in the oven until just ready to serve with the hot soup. Timing is important to produce the popping and sizzling as the soup is poured over the crusts.

(Illustrated opposite)

3 cups of rice crusts in 2 inch pieces
   (see recipe on page 32)
1/4 pound medium shrimp, shelled
1/4 pound scallops, sliced in half if large

SEAFOOD MARINADE:
1 tablespoon rice wine
1 egg white
dash of salt
1/2 cup sliced bamboo shoots or water chestnuts
4 dried mushrooms, softened and sliced
1 cup snowpeas
2 slices ginger root, minced
1 clove garlic, minced
2 scallions, sliced
1 tablespoon soy sauce
1 teaspoon chili oil
1 teaspoon sugar
1/2 teaspoon salt
1/4 teaspoon white pepper
1 teaspoon sesame oil
1 and 1/2 cups broth
2 tablespoons cooking oil

Marinate the shrimp and scallops in the wine, salt and egg white for at least half an hour. Meanwhile, prepare the other ingredients and place the fried rice crusts in the oven to stay hot.

Heat the cooking oil in a wok and stir-fry the ginger and garlic with the scallops and shrimp. When they start to change color, add the bamboo shoots, mushrooms, snowpeas, and scallions. As these vegetables are cooking, add the seasonings and then the broth. Bring the soup to a boil and pour into a heated bowl.

Immediately take the hot rice crusts and the soup to the table and pour the hot soup over the crusts to produce the sizzling display in front of your guests. Serve in individual bowls right away to retain the crispness of the crusts.

Serves 4.

Above: This is a photograph sent to us by some relatives in China.

Pork, Beef & Lamb

(Jih Ngao Yang Nguk)

PORK, BEEF & LAMB

When Chinese people refer to meat, they usually mean pork, for that is the most common form of meat. The pig has long been domesticated in China (the character for "family/home" is written pictographically as a roof over a pig). Since ancient Peking man was already acquainted with the use of fire, we can assume that culinary arts, no matter how primitive, were practiced upon this useful animal. Charles Lamb's humorous legend of the origins of roast pig may even have a grain of historic truth! In any case, the fine texture and taste of pork lends itself to Chinese cuisine, and only secondarily were beef or lamb a part of the daily fare of most Chinese homes. For the Cantonese, beef was associated with the water buffalo, which earned its keep as a beast of burden, helping with the important task of cultivating rice fields. For southerners, lamb usually meant goat (the two are written with the same character).

Within China, the Cantonese are justly famous for roast pork specialties: whole roast suckling pig, sides of roast pork, and strips of honey-roast loin meat. The dried pork sausages, lop cheang, are a popular savory addition to many dishes, as well as a side dish by itself. Various regions — Yunnan and Jinjiang, in particular — are especially noted for their cured hams.

Unlike the American practice of serving a meat as an entree to a meal, meats are usually mixed with other ingredients in a dish, and cured meats are often employed as a seasoning. This practice grew out of a rural economy in which meats were not an everyday item on the menu except for the well-to-do. Meat dishes were considered special to festive occasions, so small amounts were balanced with a higher vegetable and grain diet. It was by far a healthier way to eat. Many Americans are now coming to accept this approach to a low-meat diet.

The introduction of beef and veal into Cantonese cooking is an adaptation to foreign influence. In the United States, immigrant Chinese people early on learned to create typical Chinese meals using beef. The heavier flavor and texture of beef is readily enhanced by the use of stronger flavors like garlic, onions, oyster sauce, and fermented black soy beans. Some of the best-known Cantonese dishes include these beef and sauce combinations. Tougher cuts of beef are particularly well suited to long-simmered dishes with savory sauces.

My mother's cooking depended more upon pork in its various forms than upon beef, veal or lamb. She made soup stock from pork bones, used slices and minced pork in mixed stir-fry and steamed dishes, and sausages and ham as savory accompaniments to other dishes and soups. Her dumplings employed pork and not beef. She used beef on rarer occasions in stir-fry and stews. My own cooking borrows her pork dishes, but I have developed many beef dishes because of family and guest preferences.

I still follow Mother's technique of always marinating my meat before using it in a dish. This may have been a precaution first developed in a warm climate to prevent spoilage, but it also keeps the meat moist and flavorful. Note that after marinating, the meat sits for a while to absorb the flavor and is usually cooked first, before the vegetables.

Left: Melinda and I choosing sausages.

SISTER ANN'S SWEET AND SOUR SPARERIBS

As I mentioned previously, my mother's version of sweet and sour has tender pieces of meat (she preferred to use spare ribs) with just enough coating to seal in the juices, seasoned with a just-right blend of Cantonese pickles. Care must be taken that the sauce not be too thick. Pineapple chunks and red bell peppers can be added for color in the finished dish.
Just to illustrate the variation in Mother's legacy, my sister Ann makes this style of sweet and sour spareribs, a popular version using ketchup in the sauce.

2 pounds of spareribs (one side),with the fat trimmed and each rib cut in half

1 yellow onion, cut into chunks
1 bell pepper, cut into chunks
1 small can pineapple chunks
    (reserve juice)
1/2 cup ketchup
1 and 1/2 tablespoons sugar
1 tablespoons vinegar
1 tablespoon cornstarch mixed in
    1 tablespoon of water.

MARINADE:
1 tablespoon soy sauce
1 teaspoon salt
1 teaspoon sugar
2 teaspoons cornstarch

Place the cut-up spareribs into the marinade and set aside for 30 or more minutes.

Heat two tablespoons of cooking oil in a hot wok or skillet and brown the spareribs. After browning, lower the flame, cover and cook for about 25 minutes, stirring frequently. Remove spareribs and drain on paper toweling.

Pour out all but one tablespoon of the oil from the pan and saute the onion and pepper for two minutes. Add the pineapple chunks and mix well.

Return the spareribs to the pan and cook for a minute or two, combining well.

Combine the ketchup sugar and vinegar with the juice from the pineapples and add this to the pan, mixing to flavor all of the ingredients. Thicken the gravy by adding the cornstarch mixture and stirring until the sauce heats and the contents of the pan are well combined. Serve hot.

Serves 4 or more.

Left: This is my sister Ann and her husband, Ed Tom, in Chinatown in San Francisco on their wedding day.

SWEET AND SOUR PORK

Unlike the syrupy concoctions with heavily-coated lumps of meat which claim the name of Sweet and Sour Pork in some restaurants, my mother's version has tender pieces of meat (she preferred to use spareribs) with just enough coating to seal in the juices, seasoned with a just-right blend of Cantonese pickles. Care must be taken that the sauce not be too thick. Pineapple chunks and red bell peppers can be added for color in the finished dish.

(Illustrated opposite)

1 pound pork, cut into 3/4-inch cubes
1 tablespoon light soy sauce
1 tablespoon wine
1 teaspoon ginger juice, crushed from
　fresh ginger root
1/4 cup water chestnut flour, or
　cornstarch
1/2 cup cooking oil
1 green or red pepper, cut in bite-sized
　pieces
1 white onion, cut in segments
1 cup Cantonese pickles (recipe follows)
1 teaspoon cornstarch mixed with
　2 teaspoons chicken broth or water
1/2 cup pineapple chunks

Marinate the pork in the soy sauce, wine, and ginger juice for 30 minutes. Dredge the pieces in the cornstarch and shake off the excess.

Heat the cooking oil in a hot wok and brown the pork in several batches, draining well.

Pour out all of the oil except for one tablespoon. Stir-fry the pepper and onions for several minutes, and then add the pickles with a tablespoon of the pickling mixture. After mixing and heating, return the reserved pork pieces to the wok.
Stir to blend flavors.

If the sauce in the wok is too thin, add enough of the cornstarch mixture to thicken, and serve immediately.

Serves 4.

HOMEMADE CANTONESE PICKLES

Sweet and Sour Pork or pork spareribs is perfectly seasoned with a blend of Cantonese pickles.

(Illustrated in the background on the opposite page)

PICKLING MIXTURE:
1/2 cup of sugar
1/2 cup of rice vinegar (or white)
Pinch of salt and optional drop or two of
　hot pepper oil for a little zing

VEGETABLES TO PICKLE:
young carrots, sliced diagonally
white part of scallions, sliced in pieces,
　or whole bulbs
small florets of cauliflower
new (young) ginger root, cut in slices
　(or pieces of honeyed ginger)

Pour the pickling mixture over the cut vegetables to cover and allow to pickle overnight or longer to develop the flavor. These pickles also make a good appetizer or accompaniment to rice gruel.

OYSTER SAUCE BEEF AND BROCCOLI

As a seasoning, oyster sauce has a particular affinity with beef. The mellow flavor enhances the robust quality of the meat and contrasts well with firm-textured vegetables. Cooking hint: Use this basic recipe of seasoned beef with asparagus, bamboo shoots, cauliflower, green beans, onions, peppers, and mushrooms, or combinations of these vegetables. This technique of employing variations of a theme — oyster sauce plus beef, plus vegetables — is the way to attain variety in one's diet without too much effort.

(Illustrated opposite)

3/4 pound beef, flank or sirloin, cut into thin slices
1 pound broccoli, cut into florets, the stems peeled and sliced
1 slice ginger root, crushed
2 scallions sliced
2 tablespoons cooking oil
1/4 cup chicken broth
rice

BEEF MARINADE:
1 tablespoon each of wine, soy sauce, and cornstarch
1 teaspoon oil

SAUCE:
2 tablespoons oyster sauce
1 tablespoon soy sauce
1 teaspoon sugar
1/2 teaspoon sesame oil
1/2 teaspoon salt
1/2 teaspoon pepper

Slice and marinate the beef and set aside for half an hour. Prepare the vegetables and mix the sauce.

Heat the oil in a hot wok and stir in the beef, tossing and turning until barely done—the meat will change color. Remove the meat and reserve.

Add a little more oil if necessary to the wok and add the ginger and scallions to cook briefly before stir-frying the broccoli. Add the chicken broth and cover for a few minutes to bring the broccoli to crisp tenderness. Add the beef and the oyster sauce mixture to the pan, and stir to mix thoroughly. If the sauce is too thin, add a little cornstarch mixed in a little water to thicken. When the dish is well-heated and seasoned, remove to a serving platter and enjoy with rice.

Serves 4.

BARBECUED STEAK

My mother's occasional steak meals were an adaptation of Western cooking: Perhaps a whole piece of tenderloin steak cooked in a wok with cut up onions. She sliced it for serving in a dish with a bowl of hot water under it to keep it warm. Father liked to eat this with ketchup (named for the Cantonese term for tomato sauce—-keh-jup). I always thought it was too much meat, too plainly dressed. My own version of steak is a flank cut marinated in a Chinese-flavored barbecue sauce. The longer the piece of meat marinates, the better the flavor.

1 flank steak, with excess fat removed

MARINADE:
2 tablespoons wine or dry sherry
2 tablespoons soy sauce
2 cloves garlic, crushed
2 slices ginger, crushed
2 teaspoons sugar
1/2 tablespoon oyster sauce

Mix the marinade ingredients and place the flank steak in it for at least two hours or longer, turning several times to flavor both sides.

Grill over a charcoal fire to required doneness. Slice thinly against the grain to serve. This is just as delicious cold if you have any leftovers.

Serves 4 to 6.

GUK PAI GUT
JENNIE'S ROAST SPARERIBS

Although her very busy professional life does not allow much time for cooking, my sister Jennie still enjoys trying her hand at Chinese recipes. Here is her version of ribs marinated in a rich sauce.

2 pounds pork spareribs
2 slices ginger, minced
2 cloves garlic, minced
1/2 cup hoisin sauce
1/2 cup ground bean sauce
1 tablespoon sugar
1 teaspoon salt
1 teaspoon Kaoliang wine
   (vodka also acceptable)
1 tablespoon soy sauce

Mix together the ginger, garlic, hoisin sauce, bean sauce, sugar, salt, wine, and soy sauce. Cover the ribs with the mixture and allow to marinate for several hours or overnight.

Place the ribs on a rack over a pan of water in a 400 degree oven to roast, turning occasionally, for about an hour. The ribs will cook faster if cuts are made part of the way between each rib.

Serves 4 to 6 as part of a meal.

WOI WOK NGUK
TWICE-COOKED PORK

The cut of meat traditionally used for this spicy Sichuan dish is belly pork (fresh bacon) with its alternating layers of fat and lean meat. However, for a lower-fat version, use pork butt or shoulder. This dish probably evolved from the practice of boiling large pieces of meat for immediate eating and to keep for later meals. The plain boiled pork is sliced thinly and served with seasoned dips, and this recooked dish is given a distinctive piquancy with hot peppers.

1 1/2 pounds whole piece of pork

1 green or red sweet pepper, cut in one-inch pieces

2 garlic cloves, mashed and minced

1 slice ginger root, minced

2 scallions, sliced diagonally in 1 inch pieces

1 hot pepper, seeded and shredded

1 tablespoon ground bean sauce
   (Note: if spicy bean sauce is used, hot pepper may be omitted.)

1 tablespoon soy sauce

1 tablespoon rice wine

1 teaspoon sugar

1/2 teaspoon salt

2 tablespoons cooking oil

Bring enough water to cover the pork to a boil and add the whole piece of meat. Simmer for 35 or 40 minutes until the meat is tender. Remove from the pot and allow to cool in the refrigerator. Cut into thin slices about 1 by 2 inches. Mix together the bean sauce, soy sauce, wine, salt, and sugar in a bowl and set aside.

Heat the oil in a wok and stir-fry the garlic, ginger, scallions, and peppers. When the flavors are released, add the pork slices and the seasoning mixture, stirring to blend well. Serve hot with rice.

Serves 4 to 6.

HONG SIEU NGAU NGUK
BRAISED BEEF

The process of braising meat in a soy-based sauce is known as "red-cooking" and tougher cuts are made tender and flavorful. The meat tastes even better reheated, but can be served cold—sliced thin on an appetizer platter. I often cook large roasts and briskets in this fashion for my buffet dinners. The Chinese favor the patterning of shank beef cut thin for appetizer trays. The soy braising liquid can be strained and kept for later use; I have successfully frozen it.

1 3-pound piece of beef
   (chuck roast or brisket)

1 quart or more of water (to cover)

2 cups soy sauce

1/2 cup wine or sherry

1/2 cup sugar, rock or brown

1 tablespoon salt

2 pieces dried orange peel, softened

5 star anise

1 stick cinnamon

1/2 teaspoon Sichuan pepper

2 scallions

2 slices ginger root

1/2 teaspoon chili pepper (optional)

1 tablespoon sesame oil

Trim excess fat from the piece of beef. Bring the water with the scallions and ginger to a boil in a pot and place the beef into the water. Skim as the beef simmers, then add the soy sauce, wine, sugar, salt, orange peel, star anise, cinnamon, pepper and sesame.

Bring the pot to a boil again, and lower to heat to simmer. Cook covered for an hour and a half to two hours. The meat should be tender. Slice thin to serve, with a little of the sauce poured over the meat. The sauce can be thickened a little by boiling to reduce.

Strain the rest of the sauce and reserve. Leftover meat can be stored in the sauce.

Serves 6 or more as an appetizer.

LION'S HEAD MEATBALL CASSEROLE

Extra-large meatballs simmered with Chinese cabbage suggested the heads of lions covered with manes—hence the name for this dish. Properly cooked, the meatballs should be juicy and easily divided into more than one portion each. Have plenty of rice to soak up the broth in the casserole, which should be brought to the table to serve.

(Illustrated above)

MEATBALL MIXTURE:

1 and 1/4 pounds ground pork

3 dried mushrooms, softened and
    chopped in small pieces

1/3 cup chopped bamboo shoots, jicama
    or water chestnuts

2 slices ginger root, minced

1 scallion, minced

1/2 tablespoon dark soy sauce

1/2 tablespoons rice wine

1 teaspoon sugar

1/2 teaspoon salt

1/4 teaspoon pepper

2 tablespoons cornstarch

1 pound Chinese cabbage
    (preferably the small-sized variety)

2 or 3 tablespoons cooking oil

1/2 cup broth

1 tablespoon soy sauce

1 teaspoon sugar

1/2 teaspoon salt

1 teaspoon sesame oil

Combine all of the ingredients for the meatballs and form six large balls. If the cabbage are not the small variety, cut in large pieces. Heat the oil and brown the meatballs lightly. Remove from the wok. Next stir-fry the cabbage briefly.

Place half the cabbage on the bottom of the casserole dish, arrange the meatballs on top of the cabbage, and then cover the meatballs with the rest of the cabbage. Pour the broth and the rest of the seasonings over everything.

Cover the casserole and simmer for about 45 minutes. Thicken the broth before serving by heating with a little cornstarch mixed with water.

Serves 6 to 8.

COCKTAIL MEATBALLS

American entertainment patterns are such that I have developed some recipes for cocktail hors d'oeuvres that have a Chinese flavor but can be served on toothpicks at a party. Quantities can be increased by doubling the meat and sauce mixtures.

l pound ground meat (I use beef or veal)
1 tablespoon minced ginger root
1/4 pound water chestnuts or bamboo shoots, minced
1 tablespoon wine or sherry
1 tablespoon soy sauce
1 teaspoon of sugar and salt combined
1 egg, beaten
1/3 cup cornstarch
oil for frying

Mix the meat with ginger, water chestnuts, wine, soy sauce, sugar, salt, and egg. Shape the mixture into one-inch meatballs. Dredge the meatballs in the cornstarch, shaking off any excess.

Heat the oil in a wok or deep fryer and brown the meatballs. Remove and drain well. A lower-fat alternative is to bake the meatballs in a single layer on a baking pan in a hot oven for 8-10 minutes until done. This recipe is enough for 4 or more.

The meatballs can be served with a variety of dips, but I like to serve them in a sweet and sour sauce (see the recipe below).

SWEET AND SOUR COCKTAIL MEATBALL SAUCE

Above: Here are John and I at our wedding, with my parents and siblings. My sisters Ethel and Ann were bridesmaids.

1 and 1/2 cups chicken broth
1/4 cup sugar
3 tablespoons cider vinegar
3 scallions, chopped
1 slice ginger minced
1 tablespoons ketchup
1/4 teaspoon chili powder
1 tablespoon cornstarch, blended in a little broth

Mix these ingredients together in a saucepan and heat to boiling. As it simmers and thickens, check the seasonings and correct. Add the meatballs and heat thoroughly to serve. This dish keeps warm at a buffet table in a heated server. Provide toothpicks.

CHA SIEU
CANTONESE ROAST PORK

The signature Cantonese roast meat is usually purchased at specialty shops festooned with hanging roast ducks and pieces of barbecued pork. My parents made this a standard item on their shopping expeditions to Pittsburgh, and once they moved to San Francisco, such barbecue shops were numerous. Having spent much of my adult life far from Chinatown grocers, I have experimented with homemade versions. Here is one that I find a reasonable substitute. It is worth making in quantity, for it keeps well refrigerated for days and will also freeze. Slice it thin for appetizer trays and use it as seasoning in all sorts of other dishes, as well as in the steamed buns known as cha sieu bao.

3 pounds boneless pork loin
2 tablespoons fermented red bean curd (nahm yuh)
2 tablespoons hoisin sauce
2 tablespoons rice wine or sherry
1/4 cup maltose, or honey
1 tablespoon soy sauce
2 tablespoons crushed garlic
1 tablespoon crushed ginger
1 teaspoon five-spice powder

Cut the pork into strips about two by two inches wide and six to eight inches long. Mix the rest of the ingredients well and pour over the strips of meat in a dish that allows the pieces to lie in one layer. Make sure all sides are coated with the mixture.

Cover and marinate overnight, turning the strips several times to season well on all sides.

If possible, the strips should roast in the oven hanging from hooks from the top rack, with a pan of water below to catch the drippings. Preheat the oven to hot (about 425 degrees) and hang the strips. After 10 minutes, lower the heat to 350 degrees and continue roasting for 20 minutes. Check the meat for doneness, and brush with more of the marinade. Heat for a few minutes more or until done, and remove from oven. Allow to cool before slicing. Refrigerate or freeze extra pieces for later use.

JIENG NGUK BENG
STEAMED MEAT PATTY

This familiar standby of home cooking is never found on restaurant menus, but is remembered fondly by many as a satisfying savory accompaniment to family meals. Mother produced a great variety of these steamed patties from a pound of chopped meat flavored with such preserved condiments as salt fish, salty eggs, pickled vegetables, spiced preserves, bacon, and sausage. Not only did this stretch a small amount of meat among a large family, but the high seasoning helped to get down a great deal of rice.

The meat may be pork, chicken, beef, or veal. One simple version of Mother's was no more than a piece of ham, chopped and steamed in a dish. I am providing two of my childhood favorites: Pork patty with tea squash (cha gua) and pork patty with preserved vegetable root (jhong tsoi), which in a spicier form is known as gah tsoi from Sichuan.

1 pound chopped pork
1/3 cup tea squash, sliced in small pieces
1 teaspoon soy sauce
1/2 teaspoon salt
2 teaspoons cornstarch

Mix all of the ingredients together and press them into a shallow heat-proof dish to form a patty about half an inch thick.

Steam for about 15 to 20 minutes until done. The patty may be cut into small wedges in the dish before serving.

VARIATION WITH PRESERVED VEGETABLE:

Substitute 1/4 cup of the jhong tsoi for the tea squash and proceed as in the above recipe. A dash of sesame oil may be added before serving.

Serves 4 to 6 as part of a family meal.

MANGO BEEF

The use of tropical fruits in cooking is very much a part of Cantonese cooking. The sweet-tartness of mango is particularly well-suited to the robust flavor of beef. Select mangoes which are ripe but still firm for best results in this dish.

(Illustrated opposite)

3/4 pound beef, sliced thin
1 large mango, peeled and cut in half-inch slices
1 scallion, chopped
2 slices ginger root, shredded
1 teaspoon grated orange peel
1 tablespoon soy sauce
1 tablespoon wine
1 teaspoon sugar
1/2 teaspoon salt
1 teaspoon sesame oil
2 tablespoons cooking oil

BEEF MARINADE:
1 tablespoon of soy sauce
1 tablespoon of wine
1 tablespoon of cornstarch

Marinate the beef for at least half an hour.

Heat the oil in the wok and stir-fry the marinated meat until the color changes. Remove beef from the wok and set aside.

Add more oil if necessary and stir-fry the scallion, ginger root, and orange peel for a minute or two. Then add the rest of the seasonings to blend and return the meat to the wok, stirring to mix the flavors. Finally, add the mango slices and stir for another minute or so.

Serve hot.

Serves 4 to 6 as part of a multi-course meal.

LOTUS LEAF BUNS

Above: Here we are at a dinner in 1996, with Melinda's husband Andrew, Jennie, Tom, myself, Ann and Melinda.

Make a recipe of dough as for Barbecued Pork Buns (see page 168). After the dough has risen and formed into four-inch rounds, brush one side with sesame or other cooking oil and fold over in half. Press down gently but do not seal. The buns may be pressed in on the edge to make a lobed leaf shape.

As with the barbecued buns, place each on a square of parchment or waxed paper and set aside in a warm place to rise. Steam for 10 or more minutes until done and serve warm with the honey ham (see page 72).

Enough for about 20 buns.

PICKLED PIG'S FEET WITH GINGER

The first time I ate this dish, I was about five years old. My second sister Ann had just been born, and Mother made this dish. It is another traditional, sustaining and rebuilding food for new mothers. The calcium in the bones of the pig's feet are released by the vinegar and adds to the nutrition of this dish. Besides, it tastes so good! It is not only relished by the new mother, but it is also served to guests who come to offer congratulations upon the new arrival. More pig's feet can be added to the broth to cook up a new batch. My mother's innovation to this dish was to add apples and cider vinegar, instead of just the usual red rice vinegar.

3 or 4 pounds pig's feet, cut up into
    several pieces each
2 cups of cider vinegar
3 or 4 baking apples, cored and cut into
quarters
1/3 cup of sliced ginger root
2/3 cup rock or brown sugar
2 cups water
1 teaspoon salt

Blanch the pig's feet pieces in boiling water and rinse. Place all of the ingredients into a pot with the pig's feet. Bring to boil and simmer for an hour and a half, or until the meat begins to fall away from the bones.

This tastes even better reheated.

Serves 4 or more.

HONEY HAM

Served warm with steamed "lotus leaf" buns, this delectable treat is the Chinese equivalent of the ham biscuit of our American South, and it is dry-cured Virginia ham which best substitutes for the native Yunnan or Zhejiang varieties. The flavoring used in China is a jam made from cassia blossoms, but here I have used orange liqueur, which is more readily available and also provides a subtle aroma. This dish can also be served cold as an appetizer.

1 1/2 pounds Virginia ham in one piece
1/4 cup rock or brown sugar
1/4 cup honey
3 slices ginger root, shredded
1 tablespoon rice wine or sherry
1 tablespoon hot water
1 teaspoon orange liqueur

Scrape off any coating on the ham and soak for 40 minutes. Remove any skin and simmer the ham in water to cover for one hour.

Slice the ham into thin 1-inch by 2-inch pieces, overlap in a dish and cover with the ginger shreds, the sugar, and wine. Steam for 35 minutes.

Pour out the liquid in the dish and remove the ginger. Now mix the honey, hot water, and orange liqueur and pour over the ham slices. Steam for another half hour and serve warm with lotus buns. The ham is eaten placed inside the fold of the bun.

Serves 6 or more.

BEEF STIR-FRIED WITH TOMATOES

Beef seems to have a natural affinity with tomatoes, and this combination was a welcome addition to our family meals. Although tomatoes have been a part of Chinese cooking for centuries, it is still called fan keh (foreign eggplant).

3/4 pound beef fillet, sliced
1 pound firm ripe tomatoes
1 small onion, sliced
1 clove garlic minced
1 sliced ginger root, shredded

MEAT MARINADE:
1 tablespoon soy sauce
1 tablespoon rice wine
1 tablespoon cornstarch

SEASONING SAUCE:
2 teaspoons soy sauce
2 teaspoons oyster sauce
1 teaspoon rice wine
1 teaspoon sugar
1 teaspoon salt
dash of pepper

2 tablespoons cooking oil

Mix the sliced beef with the marinade and set aside for half an hour. If you prefer, skin the tomatoes by dipping in boiling water, deseed, and slice into segments. Prepare the other ingredients and mix the seasoning sauce.

Heat the oil in the wok and stir fry the marinated beef until the color changes. Remove the meat from wok and set aside. If necessary heat more oil in the wok (there should be at least one tablespoon) and stir in the onions, ginger root, and garlic. Next add the tomato segments along with the seasoning mixture. Stir for several minutes to cook through; then, return the meat to the wok and mix well.

Serve hot with rice or over noodles. Serves 4 as part of a meal.

BEEF STIR-FRIED WITH ONIONS

The still crisp texture of the onions gives this easy dish its special appeal. I like to use the sweet Vidalia variety, or the purple onions for their color, but onions of any variety seem to go especially well with beef. Lamb is just as delicious prepared with the same ingredients.

3/4 pound tender beef, sliced thin
2 Vidalia or purple onions
2-3 tablespoons cooking oil
1 clove garlic, crushed
1 slice ginger root, crushed
1 teaspoon sugar
1/2 teaspoon salt
dash of pepper
1 tablespoon broth
1 teaspoon sesame oil

MARINADE FOR BEEF:
1 tablespoon soy sauce
1 tablespoon rice wine
1 tablespoon cornstarch
1 teaspoon cooked oil

Marinate the beef in the soy sauce, wine, cornstarch, and oil mixture for half an hour. Slice the onions. Heat 2 tablespoons oil in the wok and stir-fry the marinated beef until the color changes. Remove meat from the wok and set aside. Add the oil to heat. Stir-fry the ginger root and garlic until flavor is released. The pieces may be removed and discarded at this point. Add the onion to the wok and stir vigorously to cook while the rest of the seasonings are added. Return the meat to the mixture and blend well. Do not allow the onions to become limp. Serve immediately.

Serves 4 to 6.

LAMB STIR-FRIED WITH PEPPERS

I learned to appreciate this spicy dish on a trip along the Silk Road in Xinjing Province, where the Muslim population ate no pork. The hot peppers in the dish provide spice and color.

(Illustrated opposite)

3/4 pound lamb, thinly sliced
1 hot red pepper, seeded and shredded
1 sweet green pepper, sliced
1 small onion, quartered and sliced
2 cloves garlic, minced
1 slice ginger root, shredded
2 or 3 tablespoons cooking oil
1 teaspoon salt
1 teaspoon sugar
1 teaspoon sesame oil

MARINADE:
1 tablespoon soy sauce
1 tablespoon rice wine
1 tablespoon cornstarch

Marinate the lamb for at least half an hour. Heat 2 tablespoons oil in a wok and stir-fry the lamb until color changes. Remove lamb from wok and set aside.

Add more oil, if necessary, to make two tablespoons and heat before adding the garlic, ginger root, onion, and hot pepper. Stir to release flavors before blending in the sweet pepper and seasonings. After a minute or so, return the lamb to the wok to mix and heat through before serving the dish hot.

Serves 4.

SPICY LAMB STEW

Lamb (or mutton) is considered too strong in taste by most Chinese, except for the Moslem or Mongol population. However, I have always liked the hearty flavor of lamb and in particular when slow-cooked in this spicy stew. Beef may be substituted in this recipe.

3/4 pound lamb, cut in 1-inch cubes
2 to 3 tablespoons cooking oil
3 carrots, cut into 1-inch pieces
3/4 pound Chinese radish, cut in 1-inch pieces
2 small onions, cut in wedges
2 slices ginger root
2 cloves garlic, mashed
1 hot pepper, or 1/2 teaspoon hot pepper flakes
1 cup broth or water
1/4 cup soy sauce
1 tablespoon hoisin sauce
1 tablespoon brown or rock sugar
1 teaspoon salt
1 teaspoon Sichuan peppercorns

MEAT MARINADE:
1 tablespoon soy sauce
1 tablespoon rice wine or sherry
1 tablespoon cornstarch

Marinate the lamb pieces for at least half an hour. Prepare the vegetables. Heat the cooking oil in a wok and brown the lamb. Remove the meat to a heavy pot or casserole. Now add more oil if necessary and stir-fry the pepper, ginger root, garlic and onions for a few minutes before placing this mixture with the lamb.

Combine the broth, soy sauce, hoisin, sugar, salt and peppercorns and pour over the lamb. Heat to a boil and then simmer covered for 25 minutes. Add the carrots and radish and continue simmering for another 25 minutes. Serve hot.

This dish reheats well and tastes even better the second day.

Serves 4 or more.

SEAFOOD

(HA THLEIN)

SEAFOOD

As a maritime province with a coastline indented by many coves, the treasures of the sea have contributed much to the Cantonese diet. In addition to the many sea creatures, from fish to shellfish, the plant life of the ocean has been harvested. It was from a type of seaweed that agar-agar provided the classic gelatin dishes, and from another variety that the taste powder known as MSG was derived. Freshwater ponds and streams also provide an abundance of aquatic life for the Cantonese wok and steamer.

Having a tradition of ever-available sea life for cooking, the Cantonese are very particular about the freshness of their seafood. The markets are full of tubs and tanks of still-swimming fish and eels, of crawling crabs and turtles and crayfish and shrimp. If a restaurant has a tank of live fish, not as decoration but as potential fare, rest assured that it is one which features Cantonese cuisine.

The very elegant banquet dishes, known as the South Seas Treasures—abalone, shark's fin, *beche-de-mer* (sea slug or sea cucumber), and bird's nest, gained their reputation in part because all are products of the South Seas or of the East Indies. All required some effort to harvest: The abalone and sea slug from diving in deep water, the birdÕs nest from high on cliff or cave walls, and the sharkÕs fin from the fierce creature, not to mention the long processing to obtain the end product. During the Ming Dynasty (1368-1644) when pirates raided the seacoast, overseas trade was prohibited and these products were not easily procured. Later, during the Qing Dynasty, the only entry was through the port of Canton (Guangzhou), where the preparation of these dishes became established as the acme of fine dining.

At my wedding banquet in a San Francisco Cantonese restaurant, all four treasures appeared as part of the menu.

Above: Here I am, shopping for fresh seafood.

However, I remember them best as very rare offerings at our family table, when Father or Mother would find time to process the bird's nest or shark's fin. Abalone does not require much processing, merely care not to overcook. Of all these, the only one I would choose to prepare myself is abalone, for it is the only one with a distinctive taste. The others are noteworthy only as expensive texture foods.

There is no doubt that seafood is favored above poultry or other meats by the Cantonese. My parents certainly were pleased by the greater abundance of fresh fish and shellfish once they moved to San Francisco, and such fare appeared regularly on their table. Mother might prepare squid, fish, or even sea slug. Father loved to buy crabs for autumn treats. Going down to Chinatown to shop might include a stop at the fish market, where Mother would look carefully at the eyes and gills of the fish for freshness.

One memorable visit, my sister and I, our three girls, and Mother toured the aquarium in Golden Gate Park. Mother's commentary as we walked from tank to tank was typical of her Cantonese view of sea life. As we gazed at the octopus waving its tentacles, she said, "They're tough, but very tasty if you pound them enough to tenderize." Some flat fish drew the comment, "Very good steamed with ginger, scallions, and a bit of cooked oil." A pair of dark bass-like fish were "Very bony, but without so many bones, they would have been eaten up long ago!" Fortunately, she spoke in Cantonese, or the guards might have decided to keep an eye on her. How I wish I had taped her remarks!

Seafood is regarded as "cool" and must be balanced in cooking with the "heat" of wine, ginger, or garlic and onion. That is why Mother used these seasonings in her fish recipes. Whether or not one believes in this system of harmonizing yin and yang, use them as an excellent means of removing any "fishy" flavors.

STEAMED FISH STEAKS WITH BLACK BEAN SAUCE

This typical Cantonese seasoning is particularly suitable for firm-fleshed saltwater fishes. I like to cook swordfish, grouper, or salmon this way.

1 and 1/2 pounds fish steaks (or fillets)
2 tablespoons fermented black beans, mashed
1 tablespoon garlic cloves, mashed
1/2 teaspoon salt
1/2 teaspoon sugar
1 teaspoon ginger root, minced
1 teaspoon wine
1 teaspoon soy sauce
2 teaspoons sesame oil or any cooked oil
1 scallion minced.

Mix together the black beans, garlic, salt, sugar, ginger root, wine, and soy sauce.

Rub the sauce mixture over the fish steaks, and place them in a heat-proof dish. Steam over high heat for about 12 minutes. Check for doneness.

Sprinkle the sesame oil and the minced scallion over the fish and serve hot.

Serves 4.

STIR-FRIED SHRIMP WITH BLACK BEAN

The Cantonese love very fresh shellfish. The fresher the shrimp, for example, the simpler the cooking required. There is a famous dish in which the live shrimp are barely marinated in wine before being eaten; another in which the shrimp are kept in a brine bath before being sauteed in the shell in seasoned oil.

When I am uncertain how long removed from the sea my shrimp are, I cook them in a black bean sauce. The texture of the shrimp is crisped by soaking in cold salted water, or by sprinkling with salt and then rinsing.

1 pound shrimp, shelled and deveined
1 tablespoon cornstarch
2 scallions, sliced diagonally
3 slices ginger root, shredded
2 tablespoons black bean sauce, mashed
2 cloves garlic, mashed
1 tablespoon wine
1/2 teaspoons sugar
1/2 teaspoons salt
1 teaspoon broth or water
2 tablespoons cooking oil

Sprinkle the shrimp with the cornstarch. Mix the black beans, garlic, wine, sugar, and salt with the broth in a small bowl.

Heat a wok. Add the oil. When hot, stir in the ginger root and scallion to release the flavors. Then add the shrimp.

Stir-fry the shrimp until pink and curled. Do not overcook. Add the sauce mixture from the bowl, and stir well to mix and heat through. Serve hot.

Serves 3 to 4 as part of a Chinese meal.

JIENG NGUI
STEAMED WHOLE FISH

This method of cooking is appropriate only with the freshest of fish, for the natural flavor of the fish is the first consideration. The minimal seasonings serve to enhance the succulence of the flesh. If possible, a banquet should include a whole fish, for fishes represent plenitude (the word for fish is a pun for the word abundance).

(Illustrated opposite)

1 whole fish, cleaned and scaled with the
    head and tail intact
      (bass or snapper are good choices)
1 dried mushroom, softened and sliced
3 slices of ginger root, shredded
2 green onions shredded
dash of salt
dash of pepper
1/2 teaspoon sesame oil or
    cooked vegetable oil
1 teaspoon light soy sauce

Wash the fish and pat dry. Slash the sides a few times through the thicker parts to allow for even cooking.

Lay the fish on its side in a heat-proof dish and arrange the mushroom slices, ginger shreds and the green onions over it. Sprinkle with salt and pepper.

Steam the fish for 10-15 minutes, depending on the size.
Before serving, drizzle the oil and soy sauce over the fish.

If you are using filets, shorten the cooking time. If the fish is large, increase the cooking time and the amount of seasonings.

JIENG HAHM NGUI
STEAMED SALT FISH

The preservation of fish by salting is an ancient technique, and the use of salt fish in the everyday diet helped provide nutritional balance to grain/vegetable-based meals. The fish can be purchased by weight or in cans packed in oil. The latter are more flavorful, and easier to prepare. The plain salted pieces must be soaked to remove some of the saltiness before cooking. This was a common savory side dish at our family meals when I was growing up. A very little dab of fish will help to get down a great amount of rice, but it is possible to detect variations in flavor among the types of salted fish, and Father was very particular about the kind he bought.

1 piece of salt fish, about 2 inches square
1 tablespoon cooked oil, if the fish is not canned

Place the fish in water to soak for a few hours if it is the plain, dried variety. Place the piece in a small heat-proof dish with the oil. If it is canned, take it out of the can, and place in a dish with some of the oil or add a little more.

Steam the fish for half an hour, or until it is softened. The canned variety just has to be heated through—about five or more minutes. Serve with plenty of rice or with rice gruel. A little will last a long time.

SWEET AND SOUR FISH

The contrast between crisp skin and the sweet-sour sauce make this a delectable dish for a special meal. It is best done with a whole fish, but fillets can also be cooked in this manner. As part of a Chinese meal, allow 1/3 pound per person.

(Illustrated opposite)

1 whole fish, cleaned and scaled, but
    with head and tail intact
1/4 cup bamboo shoots, shredded
1 carrot, shredded
1/4 cup green pepper, shredded
3 dried mushrooms, soaked to soften and
shredded
3 slices ginger root, shredded
1 teaspoon salt
ginger juice from one slice ginger root in
    1 tablespoon wine
1/4 cup cornstarch
oil for deep frying

S A U C E :
2 tablespoons broth
1 tablespoon vinegar
1 tablespoon brown sugar
1 tablespoon soy sauce
2 tablespoons ketchup

Score the fish several times on the sides. Rub the salt, ginger root juice and wine all over the fish and set aside to marinate for 20 minutes.

Dredge the fish in the cornstarch, and deep fry the fish in the hot oil, turning the fish to cook both sides evenly. Ladle oil over the fish if necessary. Remove the fish and drain. Place on warm serving platter.

Pour out all except about 1 or 2 tablespoons of the oil. Stir-fry the shredded vegetables for a few minutes. Pour in the sauce ingredients and heat well.

Pour the sweet and sour sauce over the fish and serve hot.

FISH STEAK WITH SPICY BEAN SAUCE

This easy method of preparing fish is particularly suitable for meatier fish (swordfish, garoupa, shark). The steaks can be grilled outside or under the broiler in the oven.

1 and 1/2 pounds fresh fish steaks
1/3 cup ground bean sauce
1/2 teaspoon chili paste
    (or chopped hot pepper)
1 teaspoon rice wine
dash of salt
dash of sugar
1 clove garlic, pressed
1 slice ginger root, minced or pressed

Mix together the ground bean sauce, chili paste, ginger root, garlic, salt, and pepper. Rub the mixture over the fish steaks and allow to marinate for half an hour.

Grill or broil the fish steaks for 10 or more minutes until just done, turning once. Serve immediately.

Serves 4 as part of a Chinese meal.

STEAMED CRAB

Crab eating is associated with autumn, when they are plentiful and combined with the Mid-Autumn Festival, which occurs at the full moon of the eighth lunar month. This is also chrysanthemum season. So has grown the tradition of viewing chrysanthemums and enjoying crab and wine feasts by the light of the harvest moon. I remember one San Francisco visit in the fall when my father bought a large number of crabs for a hands-on meal with various dips.

(Illustrated opposite)

1 dozen live crabs

PREPARED DIPS:
4 slices of ginger root, minced
1/3 cup rice wine vinegar
1/2 teaspoon sugar
1/4 cup oil
3 scallions, chopped
mustard sauce or chili oil (optional)

Steam the crabs about 10 minutes or until the shells turn red. The legs and extra shell may be removed and the inedible portions taken out before serving in a large platter, or at an informal meal each diner can tackle his own dismantling.

The prepared dips: Mix the ginger root with the wine vinegar and sugar. Heat the oil and pour it over the chopped scallions. Set out the mustard or chili oil if desired.

Chinese mustard can be prepared by using Colman's powdered mustard mixed in an equal amount of water with some sesame oil added.

The pieces of crabmeat are dipped in the sauces set out in small dishes around the table, or each diner may have portions of his own.

Heated rice wine is the classic drink with a crab feast, but a nice Chablis or other dry white wine will also go admirably with this meal.

Below: Here I am picking the crabs for a crab feast

LOBSTER CANTONESE

The *"dragon prawn,"* as Cantonese call their clawless lobsters, is presented with a rich sauce in this old favorite. The well-known Shrimp in Lobster Sauce has no lobster in its sauce, but is cooked in the same sauce as this lobster dish. The Chinese prefer to cook shellfish in the shell to preserve texture and flavor, making it a challenge to eat neatly!

1 live lobster, about 1 and 1/2 pounds
1 teaspoon wine and ginger juice
2 tablespoons cornstarch
1/4 pound ground pork
1 teaspoon wine
1 tablespoon soy sauce
2 teaspoons cornstarch
2 sliced minced ginger root
oil for stir-frying
1 egg, well beaten

SAUCE:
1 tablespoon fermented black bean
2 cloves garlic, minced
1 tablespoon wine
1/4 cup chicken broth
1/2 teaspoon sugar
1/2 teaspoon pepper
1/2 teaspoon salt
1/2 teaspoon sesame oil

Kill the lobster by cutting the nerve in the space between head and body. Chop the claws from the body and crack. Remove the feet, and discard the inedible parts. Cut the tail in half lengthwise and then crosswise into several pieces. Dip the pieces in wine and ginger juice and dredge in cornstarch. Marinate the ground pork in the wine, soy sauce, and cornstarch.

Cook the lobster pieces in hot oil and reserve. Heat the oil and put in the minced ginger root, then the ground pork. Stir until the pork changes color. Add in the sauce ingredients and mix well. Return the lobster to the pan and mix again. Stir in the beaten egg and continue stirring. If sauce needs thickening, add a little cornstarch mixed in water. Serve hot. The sauce is excellent over rice.

Serves 4 or more as part of a Chinese meal.

SHRIMP SAUCE PORK

If Father enjoyed salt fish as a savory, Mother preferred the distinctive flavor of shrimp paste with somewhat fatty pork. The almost lavender-colored paste made from processed shrimp is similar to anchovy paste and has about as strong a smell, but when cooked has a rich taste. Often at meals, Father would have his dish of salt fish sitting on his side of the table, while Mother had a similar dish of shrimp sauce pork on hers, probably reminding them of their own childhood dinner tables.

1/4 pound of fatty pork,
     usually fresh bacon.
1 tablespoon shrimp paste
steamed rice

Combine cut-up pieces of the fresh bacon with the shrimp paste and place in a small heat-proof dish.

Steam for half an hour, or until the fat in the meat turns translucent. Serve with rice.

YIU JHA HOH
FRIED OYSTERS

Oysters are a popular Cantonese seafood—from fresh to dried to that distinctive regional flavor of oyster sauce. Fresh oysters are especially delicious deep-fried in this crisp batter. If you have leftover batter, try dipping mushrooms or other vegetables to deep-fry as accompaniments to the oysters.

1 pound fresh shucked oysters
1 clove garlic, pressed
1/2 teaspoon ginger juice
    (from pressing ginger root)
1 teaspoon rice wine
oil for deep frying

BATTER:
2/3 cup flour
2 tablespoons cornstarch
1 teaspoon baking powder
1 teaspoon salt
1/4 teaspoon pepper
1 egg, beaten
1 teaspoon sesame oil
1/3 cup water

Soak the oysters in salted water for about 20 minutes to remove any sand or grit. Rinse and drain. Heat boiling water and pour over the oysters to blanch. Allow to drain. Sprinkle the oysters with the ginger juice, wine, and garlic put through a press. Blend the batter ingredients together until smooth. Set near the stove with the oysters while the oil for deep frying is heating. Dip the oysters in the batter to coat and place them carefully in the hot oil to brown. Drain and serve hot with various dipping sauces: prepared mustard, soy sauce and vinegar, salt and pepper.

This very rich dish will serve 4 or more as an appetizer or as part of a meal.

TENG AUH CHAU HAH
SHRIMP STIR-FRIED WITH PEAS

The combination of green peas and pale shrimp provides both color and texture with a very fresh flavor. Ideally, the peas should be sweet from the garden, but when out of season, the frozen kind will do. The shrimp, however, must be fresh.

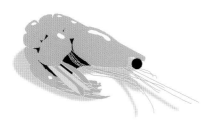

3/4 pound shelled shrimp
1/3 pound peas

SHRIMP MARINADE:
1 egg white
2 teaspoons cornstarch
pinch of salt
cooking oil for pre-cooking
    and stir-frying
1 slice ginger root, minced
2 scallions, sliced
1 tablespoon rice wine
1/2 teaspoon sugar
1/4 teaspoon salt
1/4 teaspoon chili oil
1/2 teaspoon sesame oil

If the shrimp are large, halve and cut in several pieces. Place in the marinade and let sit for at least half an hour. Parboil fresh peas for a few minutes and drain; if frozen, allow to thaw completely.

Heat about a cup of oil in the wok to about 275 degrees and cook the shrimp just enough to change color. Allow to drain thoroughly.

Leaving only 2 tablespoons of oil in the wok, raise the heat and stir-fry the ginger root and scallions for a minute or two. Add the peas, return the shrimp and combine with the all of the seasonings. Stir to finish cooking and to blend the flavors. Avoid overcooking, as the shrimp will turn tough. Serve hot.

This recipe will serve 4 or more as part of a larger meal.

STIR-FRIED FRESH SQUID

Fresh squid is a bit of trouble to clean, but Mother's style of preparing it is a special taste for any lover of seafood. Often the fish man at the market will do the cleaning for you. Care must be taken not to overcook, or the texture toughens. Scoring the larger pieces ensures quicker cooking and adds eye appeal to the dish.

(Illustrated opposite)

1/2 pound of fresh squid, cleaned
1 slice ginger root, minced
1 small white onion, cut in segments
1/4 pound mushrooms, sliced
1/4 pound water chestnuts sliced
1 green pepper, cut in pieces
1 stalk celery, sliced diagonally
1 teaspoon wine
1 slice ginger root, crushed
1 tablespoon cornstarch
1/4 cup chicken broth
1/2 teaspoon salt
1/2 teaspoon sugar
1/2 teaspoon light soy sauce
1 teaspoon sesame oil, or
1 teaspoon chili oil (optional)
2 or 3 tablespoons cooking oil

Cut the squid into squares, and score on one side in a criss-cross pattern. Marinate with the wine and ginger root, and coat with the cornstarch.

Place the broth, soy sauce, sesame oil, salt, and sugar in a bowl.

Heat two tablespoons of the cooking oil in a hot wok and stir-fry the squid for a minute or two. Remove from wok and reserve.

Add more oil to the wok, if necessary, and add the onion, green pepper, celery, mushrooms, and water chestnuts. Stir to mix and cook to tenderness. Return the squid to the pan, and pour in the seasoning sauce.

Stir well to mix in the seasonings. If sauce is too thin, add some cornstarch mixed with water to thicken. Serve hot.

Serves 4.

Below: Father and mother at Ethel and Fred's wedding in 1966.

OYSTER SAUCE ABALONE AND MUSHROOMS

Here is a dish which exemplifies smoothness of texture and taste, combining my favorite "sea treasures" with my favorite Cantonese seasoning. Abalone has become increasingly rare since my childhood, when the fresh shellfish was still available. Now the canned is the usual source. The oyster mushrooms (sometimes called "abalone mushrooms") are added to complement the slight chewiness of the abalone. Care must be taken not to overcook the abalone, for it will get tough.

1 can of abalone

1 can of oyster mushrooms, or 1/4 pound fresh (if dried, use 6 and soften)

1 slice ginger root, shredded

2 scallions, shredded

2 teaspoons rice wine

1/2 teaspoon sugar

1/2 teaspoon salt

2 tablespoons oyster sauce

1 teaspoon sesame oil

1 tablespoon cooking oil

2 teaspoons cornstarch, mixed with equal amounts of broth or water

Reserve the juice from the can of abalone. Slice the abalone about 1/4 inch thick each piece.

In a wok, heat the oil and stir-fry the ginger root and scallions. Add the mushrooms and stir to cook. Pour in 1/4 cup of the reserved abalone liquid with the wine, sugar, salt, oyster sauce, an sesame. Add enough of the cornstarch mixture to thicken the sauce. As it thickens, add the abalone and heat thoroughly. Serve hot over a plate lined with lettuce or other leafy green.

Scallops or oysters can be substituted in this dish, but they would be added to the wok with the mushrooms to cook for a longer period than the abalone.

Serves 4 or more.

GINGER STIR-FRIED FISH

Without heavy sauce or oiliness, this simple dish brings out the tenderness and natural flavor of the fresh fish, with color and texture contrast provided by the carrot and mushrooms.

1 pound fish fillets, cut in thin slices

1 tablespoon rice wine

dash of salt

1 egg white

1 tablespoon cornstarch

1 tablespoon young ginger root, shredded

1 scallion, shredded

1 small carrot, thinly sliced

5 or 6 fresh mushrooms, sliced

2 tablespoons cooking oil

1/2 teaspoon sugar

1/2 teaspoon salt

dash of pepper

2 tablespoons broth

1 teaspoon sesame oil (optional)

Place the sliced fish in a bowl. Sprinkle with the wine and salt, mix with the egg white, and dust with the cornstarch.

Heat the oil in a wok and toss in the ginger root and scallion to cook for about a minute before adding the fish to stir until the slices change color.

Add the carrots and mushrooms to the wok with the the seasonings and broth. Stir for a few minutes more to cook through. If you wish, add the sesame oil just before serving.

Serves 4 as part of a Chinese meal.

BATTER FRIED FISH FILLETS

Delicate fillets of smaller fish can be fried in a light batter to preserve their fine texture and flavor. The secret is in the fluffy batter and the moderate temperature of the oil to keep from browning the batter and hardening the fish pieces.

1 and 1/2 pounds fresh fillets from small
    fish (flounder, sole, trout)
1 tablespoon rice wine
dash of salt
1 tablespoon cornstarch
oil for deep-frying

B A T T E R :
2 egg whites, well beaten
1/2 cup sifted flour
1/4 teaspoon white pepper
dash of sugar
dash of salt

Sprinkle the fish fillets with the rice wine and salt. Dust each piece with cornstarch. After beating the egg white until stiff, fold in the flour and seasonings to blend.

Heat oil for deep-frying in a wok to about 300 degrees. Dip each fillet into the batter to coat before sliding carefully into the hot oil. Turn to cook until golden. Then remove the pieces to drain well and keep warm until all the fish has been cooked. Serve hot.

Serves 4 to 6 as part of a multi-course meal.

SPICY SEAFOOD STIR-FRIED WITH PEPPERS

The spiciness of this seafood and vegetable combination can be modified by reducing the amount of hot pepper in the seasoning. I particularly like to use scallops in this dish because the texture and sea flavor contrast so well with the piquancy of the pepper.

1 pound shrimp, scallops, and/or squid
1/2 cup sliced fresh mushrooms
1 sweet red or green pepper, cut in
    one-inch pieces
1 hot pepper, seeded and shredded
2 scallions, cut in one-inch segments
1 clove garlic, minced
2 slices ginger root, shredded
2-3 tablespoons cooking oil

M A R I N A D E :
1 tablespoon rice wine
1/2 teaspoon salt
2 teaspoons cornstarch

S A U C E :
1 tablespoon light soy sauce
1 tablespoon rice wine
1 tablespoon broth
1/2 teaspoon cornstarch
1 teaspoon sugar
1/2 teaspoon salt
dash of pepper

Prepare the seafood—wash, and cut up if large—and marinate for at least half a hour. Mix the sauce together in a bowl and cut up the vegetables. Heat oil in a wok to a moderate temperature and stir-fry the seafood until the color changes. Remove from wok and set aside.

Add more oil, if necessary, to make about 2 tablespoons to heat in the wok. Stir-fry the hot pepper, scallions, ginger root, and garlic together to release the flavors; add the mushrooms and sweet pepper and stir for a few minutes. The seasoning sauce is next mixed in to thicken a little before the seafood is returned to the wok to heat through. Serve hot.

Serves 4.

PHOENIX TAIL SHRIMP

These deep-fried morsels are wonderful for either family fare or guest meals. Make the latter more festive with the addition of a handful of nuts (walnuts or pecans) deep-fried and arranged around the shrimp.

(Illustrated opposite)

1 pound large shrimp in the shell
1/2 teaspoon salt
1 tablespoon rice wine
1 tablespoon cornstarch
oil for deep-frying

BATTER:
1 cup flour
1 tablespoon baking powder
1 cup water

SEASONED SALT:
1 tablespoon salt
1/2 teaspoon ground Sichuan peppercorns.

Shell the shrimp except for the tails. Devein and butterfly so that the shrimp will cook more evenly. Sprinkle the salt and wine over the pieces and dust with the cornstarch.

Sift the flour with the baking powder and mix in the water gradually to make a smooth batter.

Heat oil for deep-frying (375 degrees). Picking the shrimp up by the tail, dip each in the batter and slide carefully into the hot oil a few at a time. Remove when they turn golden and drain well. Keep warm until all are fried and serve immediately.

The usual accompaniment to deep-fried shrimp is a seasoned salt. Make it by heating together a tablespoon of salt with 1/2 teaspoon of ground Sichuan peppercorns.

Serves 4 to 6.

Below: This is me on the right with daughters Melinda and Tania, and niece Cathy. The special occasion was Cathy's wedding banquet.

HAPPY UNION OF DRAGON AND PHOENIX

Literally, the name for this dish is "Dragon Flies As Phoenix Dances," to represent the felicity of male and female in joyful harmony. This makes an elegant selection for an anniversary or wedding dinner. The addition of the green vegetable provides color contrast, often referred to as a "Jade Bower" in which the happy couple gambols.

(Illustrated opposite)

3/4 pound skinless chicken breast, sliced
3/4 pound shrimp, shelled and veined
1/2 pound broccoli florets, briefly
    blanched in boiling water
2 scallions sliced
2 slices ginger root, mashed
1 clove garlic, mashed

CHICKEN MARINADE:
1 tablespoon rice wine
1 egg white
1 tablespoon cornstarch
dash of salt

SHRIMP MARINADE:
1 tablespoon rice wine
1/4 teaspoon salt
1 teaspoon cornstarch
1 cup cooking oil

SEASONING MIXTURE:
1 tablespoon soy sauce
1 tablespoon oyster sauce
1 teaspoon sugar
1/2 teaspoon salt
dash of pepper
1/4 cup broth
1/2 teaspoon cornstarch

Blend the marinade ingredients for the chicken, add the slices and mix well. In another bowl, add the shrimp to its marinade. And set both aside for at least half an hour while blanching the broccoli and preparing other ingredients.

Heat the oil in a wok to about 300 degrees and cook the chicken pieces and the shrimp separately for just long enough to change color—about half a minute. Drain well. Remove oil from the wok, leaving just two tablespoons.

Add ginger root, garlic, and scallions to the oil and stir to release flavors. Ginger and garlic may be removed at this point.

Return the chicken pieces and the shrimp to the wok, stirring to heat and finish cooking. The blanched broccoli is now added to blend, along with the seasoning mixture. Keep stirring to mingle flavors and allow the sauce to thicken a little. Serve hot.

Serves 4 or more.

Left: The whole family at niece Cathy's wedding. Happy Union of Dragon and Phoenix is a popular dish for wedding celebrations.

THE MID-AUTUMN MOON FESTIVAL BANQUET

Next to the New Year, the Mid-autumn Moon Festival is the most important traditional holiday celebrated by Chinese. On the fifteenth day of the eighth lunar month, the full moon is usually large and bright. At this point in the agricultural cycle, everyone celebrates the fruits of a good harvest — very much like Thanksgiving — with a great family feast and viewing of the moon. All sorts of legends are associated with the moon. There is a Moon Goddess named Chang O who became an immortal when she stole and drank the elixir of immortality. She fled to the moon, where she lives in a palace and shares space with a hare who mixes ingredients for the elixir with a mortar and pestle. During the Moon Festival the Moon Goddess is said to grant the dearest wishes of the worthy. Traditionally, this has been a women's holiday because the moon is symbolic of the feminine principle, just as the sun represents the male principle. Women set out offerings to the full moon on this night and make their prayers, but my mother simply told us to enjoy the fullness of the moon and wish for good fortune.

I enjoyed this festival because we had mooncakes. These very rich cakes were rounded like the full moon and the dough crusts held a variety of fillings. Each region of China had its own types of mooncakes, but the Cantonese had the most diverse kinds; mixed nuts, preserved fruits, sweet bean paste — sometimes with a salted egg yolk in the center, ground lotus seeds and almonds, mincemeat, and even some with flaky crusts. These were at one time made in homes,

but nowadays most people buy them in bakeries. My favorite has a flaky crust and is filled with sweetened winter melon. Father liked the ones with many varieties of nuts and seeds. Most were so rich that we cut them into small bites so that we could taste more than one. When we lived in Canonsburg, my father would buy our mooncakes in Pittsburgh; when the family moved to San Francisco, the cakes were more readily available. They are purchased in sets of four or more in colorful boxes and presented to friends and relatives as gifts. We children often were given cookies shaped like fish or buddhas made of a kind of gingerbread during this holiday.

Popular lore relates a tale of mooncakes used in the overthrow of the oppressive rule of the alien Mongol Dynasty in the 14th century. Since the seasonal cakes were made at home and given as gifts, messages with details of a general uprising were sent baked in mooncakes and circulated among the rebels.

Packages of mooncakes from my parents when I lived far from them always reminded me of the flavors of this family holiday, and each bite of the delicacies would bring back the memory of splendid meals made from the harvest of fall vegetables, nuts and meats. This was the time of year for hearty soups and simmered dishes. Each season has its symbolic flower and the chrysanthemum is the flower of autumn. A Fall Chrysanthemum Festival is still celebrated in my parents native province of Guangdong. There is even a tonic tea made entirely from dried chrysanthemum blossoms, and petals of the flower are often scattered in the broth of a Cantonese version of the fire pot.

The Moon Festival is blended in my mind with our childhood Halloween pumpkins, of my mother's inventive use of leftover pumpkin in a typical Cantonese dish, and her unique version of roast turkey with fermented bean paste for Thanksgiving. This American holiday seemed so very Chinese to my parents, for it featured a great feast and a family reunion. Since it was a time when they had a holiday from work, there was often more time for preparation of a special meal. As a result, we had family celebrations of Thanksgiving also, but with all Chinese food.

The fall is also crab season, the occasion for crab feasts served with warming sauces of ginger, sugar, and wine to balance the "coldness" of the crab. Alcoholic beverages are always drunk with food in China. They are made from rice, sorghum, and other grains and flavored with herbs and other condiments. Mother did not drink, but Father's favorite was a sorghum based herbal liquor with a caramel flavor called Ng Gha Peh. I liked the shape of the bottle that held this drink and the aroma of the dark liquid when he uncorked the bottle. He took a drink only during special feasts such as this one. Mother did use alcohol in her marinades, but cooking always allows the alcohol to evaporate, leaving only the flavor.

The photograph on the facing page includes the following: Steamed Crab (see the recipe on page 84), Mother's Thanksgiving Turkey (page 112), Pumpkin with Dried Shrimp (page 142), mooncakes with salted egg yolk and sweetened bean paste filling, a bottle of Ng Gha Peh, and chrysanthemums.

POULTRY

(GAI AHP)

POULTRY

The Cantonese have high regard for all kinds of poultry in cooking. Rural households raised chickens, ducks, and geese for family consumption, as well as for the marketplace; their eggs are a welcome by-product. Game birds, considered more potent in nutrition than the domesticated fowl, are eagerly sought for special dishes.

In the yin-yang balance of elements, the rooster represents yang to a high degree; therefore, chicken is often matched with yin foods—seafood, greens—to produce a dish harmonious in elements and in color. Such symbolic associations surround all of the poultry family. Pairs of Mandarin ducks represent marital fidelity, and squabs display parental care. In decorations and works of art, the use of ducks, roosters, and squab are common.

When poultry is cooked, use is made of all edible parts of the bird. So it is that even the feet of chickens and ducks are made into distinctive dishes: braised "phoenix claws" refer to chicken feet, and one popular cold dish which accompanies Peking duck is "webs in mustard sauce." However, in this country, except when my mother purchased a live chicken, we did not have chicken feet dishes. Nostalgic diners must patronize Chinatown dim sum establishments to indulge in this traditional offering. I remember wind-dried ducks (lap ahp), which were used to season vegetable dishes in much the same way as wind-dried sausages. There was even a sausage made from duck livers, which had a richer taste than the wine-cured pork ones.

When I was young, chickens were still considered a special dish. When it came to picking out fresh chickens, Mother was the expert. When the farmer brought several live fowl for her selection, she looked at the eyes for brightness and felt the flesh for plumpness. I still recall the smell of wet feathers as I helped to pluck the chicken, but it was always worth it for the delicate flavor of her white cut chicken dipped in our choice of sauces. Mother always dismissed the thought of using frozen poultry, "moh mei (no taste)." This simple dish has flavor only when prepared with a fresh chicken, and it was a special treat on Saturday night after the work week was over. One year, during the meat rationing of World War II, we raised our own chickens. It was my chore to feed them, and I was very glad when one of this pecking, cackling flock went into the pot or was carried off in a squawking bundle by a visiting relative.

Now, I am pleased at the relatively low cost of chickens, for there are so many ways to prepare this tender meat! I well remember my parents' cooking all kinds of traditional recipes—from simple boiled chicken to elaborate minced and flavored delicacies. It is no surprise that so many festival meals feature chicken, duck, or other fowl, or that rich chicken broth is the base for

great banquet offerings. In this country, poultry is quite tender, so for braised dishes it is better to use roasters rather than fryers. For a stir-frying dish with chicken slices, breast meat is the easiest to use.

The advantage of buying a whole chickens is that the bones, back, and neck can go into the making of rich broth. Liver and giblets can be braised or go into soup.

In Guangdong, duck dishes are probably as common as chicken, so that many of the same recipes apply, especially the braised and the ones using richer sauces. In this country, ducks are relatively expensive, so that I usually have them for special occasions.

Above: Ann and I with a Peking Duck meal we prepared.

BAK JAHM GAI
WHITE CUT CHICKEN

The very simplicity of this recipe requires that only the freshest chicken be used for flavor, and that care be taken not to boil it too long, for that will toughen the meat. This was the most common method my mother used in cooking a freshly killed chicken on Saturday nights in Canonsburg.

1 fresh chicken, about 3 pounds, dressed
1 scallion
2 slices ginger root
1 teaspoon sesame oil

Place chicken in a pot with enough water to cover. Bring to a boil and skim. After five or six minutes of boiling, cover the pot and turn off the heat.

Allow the chicken to continue cooking in the hot water without uncovering the pot for an hour or more.

When ready to serve, remove the chicken from the pot and rub it with the sesame oil. Cut into serving pieces and arrange on a platter. My mother cut it the classic way, using a cleaver through the bones, and reformed the shape of the chicken on the serving plate. I generally debone the meat for easier eating, throwing the carcass back into the cooking water to make a rich broth.

Small dishes of seasonings are served with this plain chicken: soy sauce, oyster sauce, mustard with a bit of vinegar mixed in, mixed salt and ground Sichuan peppercorns, and red pepper sauce. My favorite seasoning is a mixture of sesame, soy sauce, and oyster sauce.

Serves 4 to 6.

Leftovers are good in mixed salads.

SIH YIU GAI
SOY SAUCE CHICKEN

Here is a seasoning broth with a soy sauce base which can be used to cook more than one chicken in succession. It can be strained and saved in the refrigerator or freezer for future use. Parts of chicken and giblets can be seasoned in this manner, also.

Right: Commercially-prepared soy sauce.

1 young chicken, washed and patted dry
1/2 teaspoon sesame oil

SAUCE MIXTURE:
2 cups broth or water
2 cups soy sauce
1/2 cup sugar (preferably rock sugar)
1 tablespoon wine or sherry
2 slices ginger root, crushed
2 scallions cut into two-inch pieces
4 star anise
1 piece dried orange peel, soaked to soften

Bring the sauce mixture to a boil in a pot, and add the chicken. Simmer for 30 to 40 minutes, turning the chicken to ensure even seasoning on all sides.

When the chicken is done, remove from the sauce and coat with the sesame oil. Cut into serving pieces and place on a platter. May be eaten warm or cold.

Serves 4 or more.

ANN'S STEAMED CHICKEN

This is my sister's version of a family-style steamed chicken dish, in which the dried and preserved ingredients combine to infuse the chicken pieces with flavor, producing a savory accompaniment to plain rice.

1/2 pounds chicken, cut into bite-sized
    pieces (with or without bones)
1 tablespoon wine
2 and 1/2 tablespoons soy sauce
1 teaspoon salt
1/2 cup golden needles (dried lily buds),
    soaked to soften
6 to 8 dried red dates, soaked to soften
4 to 5 dried black mushrooms,
    soaked to soften
1/2 Chinese sausage (lap cheang),
    cut into small slices

Marinate the chicken pieces in the wine, soy sauce, and salt.

Remove the tough stems from the mushrooms and slice. Remove the seeds from the dates and cut in halves or thirds. Nip off the hard tip of the lily buds and tie into a knot to keep the buds whole and add to the appearance of the dish.

Mix all of the prepared ingredients together and place in a shallow heat-proof dish. Steam for half an hour, or until the chicken is cooked. Serve hot.

With other dishes, serves 4 or more.

SPICY CHICKEN SALAD

This is a milder Cantonese version of a popular Sichuan cold chicken dish known as bang bang ji. I find that it is a good recipe to use up leftover plain chicken, but it is also an excellent buffet offering or picnic dish.

2 chicken breasts
2 cups shredded lettuce
1 medium cucumber, shredded
2 slices ginger root, finely slivered
1/2 cup cilantro leaves (optional)

DRESSING:
2 tablespoon sesame butter, or peanut
    butter
1 tablespoon dark rice vinegar
1 tablespoon soy sauce
1 tablespoon rice wine or sherry
2 teaspoons sugar
2 teaspoons chili oil, or more if you like
    it spicier
2 teaspoons minced or pressed garlic
1/4 teaspoon Sichuan pepper
2 teaspoons sesame oil
1 tablespoon broth or water

If the chicken is not cooked, steam for 10 minutes. Cut or tear into strips.

Make a bed of the shredded lettuce, place the shredded cucumber over the lettuce, and the chicken on top with the ginger sprinkled over it.

Mix the dressing ingredients thoroughly. This is easily done in a blender. When ready to serve the salad, drizzle the dressing over the chicken and vegetables and mix gently.

Serves 4 or more as a buffet dish.

CHICKEN WITH PEPPERS AND CASHEWS

This dish has a colorful eye appeal as well as delicious flavor — a sure hit with family and guests alike.

1/2 pound chicken, diced
1 cup diced red or green bell pepper
1/2 cup cashews
1/2 cup water chestnuts, jicama,
    or bamboo shoots, diced
3 dried mushrooms, softened and diced
1 slice ginger root, minced
1/4 cup oil for frying

CHICKEN MARINADE:
1 egg white
1 tablespoon cornstarch
pinch of salt

SAUCE MIXTURE:
1 tablespoon stock
1 tablespoon soy bean paste
    (or hoisin sauce)
1 tablespoon rice wine
1/2 teaspoon sugar

Marinate the chicken in the egg white, cornstarch, and salt and set aside.

Heat the oil in the wok and toast the cashews. Remove and drain the nuts. Next, cook the chicken in the oil until the color changes. Remove the chicken and drain.

Pour out all except for about one table-spoon of the oil. Cook the ginger root and then the rest of the vegetables. Add the sauce mixture and the chicken. Stir to mix well and heat thoroughly. Stir in the cashews before serving hot.

Serves 3 to 4 as part of a meal.

CHICKEN LIVERS AND ONIONS

Chinese are very appreciative of organ meats, which are considered delicacies, as well as sources of high nutrition. Chicken livers or pork livers are often cooked with members of the onion family, a very good balance of flavors, as well as yin and yang.

1 pound livers, cut into bite-size pieces
2 tablespoons cooking oil
2 onions or leeks, sliced
1/2 teaspoon sugar
1/2 teaspoon salt
1/4 teaspoon pepper
1 teaspoon sesame oil
1 tablespoons wine

MARINADE:
1/2 teaspoon salt
1 tablespoon soy sauce
1 tablespoon rice wine

Marinate the liver in the salt, soy sauce, and rice wine. Heat oil in the wok and stir-fry the marinated liver until just done. Remove and reserve.

Add more oil if necessary and cook the onions, adding the sugar, salt, and pepper. Return the livers to the pan. Drizzle in the sesame oil and wine and mix well before serving hot.

Serves 3 to 4.

VELVET CHICKEN

The "velveting" of chicken is a process of finely mincing the meat in order to tenderize it, and fluffing it with egg white to create a melt-in-the-mouth quality similar to that of the French quenelles. Traditionally, the chicken meat is reduced to a pulp — using a cleaver to scrape and mince—while removing any tendons or membranes. In the modern kitchen, a food processor or blender can make short work of this process. The resulting light pulp is then poached to near doneness and then used in many elegant dishes, including the great banquet soups. My father added it to his whole winter melon creation and to his sharks fin broth. Velvet chicken was a favorite dish of the last Empress Dowager.

1 skinless, boneless chicken breast
1 tablespoon cold water or broth
1/2 teaspoon salt
1 tablespoon wine
1 tablespoon cornstarch
2 egg whites, beaten
2 teaspoons oil

If you are mincing with a cleaver, combine scraping and chopping with removing any clinging membranes, while adding the cold water and the salt. When you have reduced the meat to a fine pulp, mix in the wine, cornstarch, egg whites, and then the oil. Set in the refrigerator to cool.

If you are using a food processor, cut the breast into smaller pieces, add the water and salt, and blend. Next add the rest of the ingredients and puree the mixture. Set aside to cool in the refrigerator.

The velvet chicken can be poached in oil or water, but I prefer to use water to reduce the total fat in the dish. Moreover, water poaching allows the velvet chicken to be refrigerated for a day or two before using.

Heat water in a pot or wok and allow to simmer (not a rolling boil). Form pieces of the chicken with a spoon and slip into the water. Suit the size of your pieces to the final dish you plan to prepare. For soups, I prefer slightly ovoid pieces made with a teaspoon. A melon baller can form rounds, and larger shapes can be made with tablespoons. Turn the pieces in the water to ensure even cooking. They will float to the surface when done; do not overcook, for they just need to be ready to add to the final dish to finish cooking. Remove and drain. Refrigerate if they are not being used immediately.

Above: Here are Melinda and I shopping for oranges in San Francisco. They will play an important part in decorating the table for Chinese New Year's.

CANTONESE ROAST DUCK

The richly colored and aromatic ducks hanging in Chinatown meat shops are usually professionally cooked. However, if one is far removed from sources of supply, this homemade version is also delicious.

1 five-pound Long Island duckling, dressed (Chinese people prefer the head to be left on)
2 scallions

SEASONING SAUCE:
1 tablespoon fermented red bean (or ground bean paste)
2 tablespoons wine or sherry
1/2 teaspoon five-spice powder
1 dried orange peel, soaked to soften
1 clove of garlic, mashed
2 slices ginger root, crushed
2 teaspoons sugar
1/2 teaspoon Sichuan pepper

GLAZE FOR DUCK:
1/3 cup maltose or honey
1/2 tablespoon wine
2/3 cup water

Wash the duck and pat dry. Rub with some salt inside and out. Tie up the neck (or neck opening) so that seasoning sauce will not spill out when duck is hung upside down. Mix the seasoning sauce and rub it inside the duck. Now sew up the lower cavity opening.

The ducks are usually hung by their feet, but most dressed ducklings in this country lack feet, so tie the duck with twine so that it can be hung upside down. Bring a pot of about a quart of water with the scallions to a boil and scald the duck, using a ladle to pour water all over the duck. Discard the water.

Hang the duck on a hook to dry. The skin will have puffed up and become smoother. When the skin is dry, bring the glaze ingredients to a simmer, and coat the duck. Allow the duck to dry again. The drying can be hastened by using a fan.

Preheat the oven to about 400 degrees. Hang the duck upside down from the highest rack, with a pan underneath to catch the drippings. Some water in the pan will prevent the oil from burning. Roast for 15 minutes, and then reduce the setting to 350 degrees. The total cooking time should be about one hour, but check for doneness.

When you remove the duck from the oven, pour out the juice inside the cavity and reserve as a sauce to pour over the pieces of duck on the serving platter. A popular embellishment for roast duck is to add pineapple pieces or litchee to the sauce with a bit of the pineapple juice. The duck is good hot or cold, and leftover pieces can be used to flavor stir-fried dishes of vegetables or noodles.

Serves 4 or more.

Above: Ducks, chickens and pork ribs hanging in a Chinese market in San Francisco. The recipe on this page will help you to prepare a duck like those on display here.

JIH BAU GAI
PACKAGED CHICKEN

A fun way to serve tidbits of chicken to guests as an appetizer or as part of a Chinese dinner is to present seasoned pieces of meat in envelopes of parchment or edible rice paper. The packets are deep-fried, but the contents are tender without being oily.

(Illustrated opposite)

1 pound of chicken, cut into slices
1/2 pound ham, cut into smaller slices
1/2 cup bamboo shoots, sliced
1/2 cup water chestnuts, sliced
6 dried mushrooms, softened and sliced
3 scallions, slivered
   (or leaves of cilantro)
parchment paper
oil for deep-frying

SAUCE:
2 slices of ginger root, minced
1 tablespoon rice wine
1 teaspoon sugar
1/2 teaspoon salt
2 tablespoons oyster sauce
1 teaspoon sesame oil

Mix the sauce ingredients in a bowl and place the chicken pieces in to marinate. Prepare the other ingredients.

Use 4 1/2- or 5-inch square pieces of parchment paper. Place a piece of chicken with some of the ham, bamboo shoots, water chestnuts, mushroom, and scallions near one corner of the square. Fold the parcel like an envelope by turning up the lower corner over the filling, and then the sides. Fold over and tuck the upper corner into the flap. If necessary, seal the opening with egg white or some cornstarch in water mixture—particularly if you are using rice paper.

Heat the oil and deep-fry the packets a few at a time for about 4 or 5 minutes each. Drain well, and keep warm while you finish frying all of the batches.

If you are using rice paper, the packets can be eaten as is; each guest can open his own parchment package at the table, or the host can slit the openings for greater ease in eating.

Serves 6 or more as part of a meal.

Above: This is a family portrait from the 1920s of relatives who lived in San Francisco. She was related to mother, and he was related to father. I stayed with them frequently while I was attending Stanford University.

MINCED SQUAB IN LETTUCE CUPS

It was just after the war that one of Father's friends supplied him with some squab, and he produced this elegant banquet dish for a special meal. If squab or quail is not available, this dish can also be made with Cornish hen or other similar fowl. Quail are much prized not only for their tender meat but also for their eggs, which are used to embellish special braised dishes and soups.

(Illustrated opposite)

3/4 pound of squab meat, minced
1 head of crisp lettuce
2 smoked oysters, chopped
1/4 cup bamboo shoots, chopped
1/4 cup water chestnuts, chopped
4 dried mushrooms, chopped
2 cloves garlic, minced
2 slices ginger root, minced
2 scallions chopped
oil for cooking

MARINADE:
2 teaspoons wine
1 teaspoon salt
1 tablespoon cornstarch

SEASONING:
1 tablespoon oyster sauce
1 tablespoon soy sauce
1 tablespoon wine
1 teaspoon sugar
1/2 teaspoon salt
pinch of pepper
1 teaspoon sesame sauce

Place the minced squab in the marinade and set aside for half an hour. Prepare the other chopped ingredients. Separate the leaves of lettuce, wash, and allow to crisp. Mix the seasoning in a small bowl.

Heat oil in a wok and stir-fry the squab meat. Remove and reserve.

Next stir-fry the minced garlic and ginger. Then mix in the bamboo shoots, water chestnuts, and mushrooms. Add the scallions, smoked oysters, and the seasoning mixture, stirring the mix. Return the squab meat to the wok, and stir well to heat through and absorb the seasonings.

Serve the squab mixture on a heated platter along with a plate of the crisp lettuce leaves. Each diner places a portion of the squab into a lettuce leaf and rolls it into a neat package to eat by hand.

Serves 4 to 6.

Above: Here are Andrew and Melinda, about to enjoy a casserole served in a lettuce cup like that which we use to serve the Minced Squab.

STEAM-POT CHICKEN CASSEROLE

This special Yunnan chimney pot, in which steam rises through an internal funnel into the covered pot and infuses the chicken with the flavors of the other ingredients and creates the rich broth for the dish, is an ingenious variation on steamers which have been a part of Chinese cuisine since Neolithic times. Two-piece earthenware steamers have been dug up in 6,000-year-old sites of early settlements. Without a steam-pot, this casserole can also be made in a regular casserole by adding two cups of chicken broth to the ingredients and simmering for 35 or 40 minutes, but the flavor is less delicate.

1 young chicken,
   cut up into serving pieces
1/4 pound ham, cut into cubes
2 slices ginger root
4 dried mushrooms, softened
   and hard stems discarded
1/2 cup bamboo shoots, sliced
1/4 cup rice wine
1 small piece ginseng (the Yunnanese
   often use a local herb)

Place all of the ingredients into the pot, and cover. Place the entire pot on a rack inside a larger pot with steaming water. Cover and steam for about an hour. I use a pot full of water and set the covered steam-pot over it, as the water pot is narrower in diameter than the steam-pot, This forces all of the steam into the upper pot through the chimney and allows the broth to accumulate more quickly to cook the casserole contents.

The chicken is served from the pot at the table. Serve each guest some of the chicken with broth and flavorings.

Serves 4 to 6.

SALT-ROASTED CHICKEN

This is a recipe which comes from the salt fields along the coast of Guangdong, but is one unique method of roasting which does not require an oven. The chicken is cooked by heating the surrounding salt in a pot on top of the fire or stove; however, the chicken is not especially salty and the salt is still usable. I remember my father making chicken by this method in Canonsburg, where we did not have an oven.

1/3 pound chicken
8 pounds sea salt
2 scallions
2 slices ginger root
2 tablespoons wine vinegar
2 tablespoons cooked oil

Heat a quart of water in a pot with the scallions, ginger root, and wine vinegar. Scald the chicken in the water, ladling water over the chicken to make sure all of the surface is covered. Discard the water, and allow the chicken to dry by hanging in a cool place.

Paint the skin of the chicken with the cooked oil, and cover the chicken with cheesecloth or parchment.

Meanwhile, heat about one-third of the salt in a pot large enough to hold the chicken with room to surround it with salt. Heat the rest of the salt in another pot.

Form a well in the lesser amount of salt, but allow at least a 1 1/2-inches of salt on the bottom. Place the wrapped chicken in this well, and pour the rest of the heated salt on top of the chicken so that it is entirely surrounded.

Cover and cook for an hour or until tender. Remove the chicken from the salt and cut into serving pieces to use with various dips.

Serves 6.

CHICKEN STIR-FRIED WITH MUSHROOMS

The smooth compatibility of chicken slices with fresh mushrooms has made this combination a perennial favorite at Cantonese tables. Regular soy sauce may be substituted for the mushroom soy sauce, but the latter intensifies the flavor of this dish.

3/4 pound boneless chicken, thinly sliced
1/2 pound fresh mushrooms, sliced
2 scallions, sliced
1 clove garlic, crushed
1/4 cup water chestnuts or bamboo
   shoots, sliced
2 teaspoons mushroom soy sauce
1 tablespoon rice wine
1 teaspoon sugar
1/2 teaspoon salt
2-3 tablespoons cooking oil

CHICKEN MARINADE:
1 egg white
1 tablespoon cornstarch
dash of salt

Mix the chicken slices with the egg white, cornstarch and dash of salt and set aside to marinate for at least half an hour. Mix together the mushroom soy sauce, wine, sugar, and salt and set aside.

Heat the oil in the wok to moderate and stir-fry the chicken until the color changes. Remove from wok. Add more oil, if necessary to heat, and stir-fry the garlic, scallions, water chestnuts and sliced mushrooms for a few minutes. Add the seasoning mixture and the reserved chicken and stir well to finish cooking. Serve hot.

Serves 4.

CHICKEN AND CHESTNUT CASSEROLE

Here is a festive dish for winter meals—full of rich flavors with mellow chestnuts complementing the pieces of tender chicken. The sauce is seasoned with the concentrated essence of ginger, dried mushrooms and orange peel.

2 pounds chicken,
   preferably thighs or legs
1 pound shelled chestnuts
10 dried mushrooms, rehydrated
1/2 cup bamboo shoots, either fresh or
dried (rehydrated)
3 slices ginger root
1 piece dried orange peel, rehydrated
2 tablespoons cooking oil

4 tablespoons soy sauce
2 tablespoons rice wine or sherry
1 and 1/2 cups broth
1 tablespoon sugar
1/2 teaspoon salt

Cut the chicken through the bone into two-inch pieces. The dried ingredients should be rehydrated by soaking until soft. Shred the ginger root, remove stems from the mushrooms, and slice the bamboo shoots. Boil and peel the chestnuts. If using dried chestnuts, soak until soft and drain.

Heat the oil in the wok and brown the chicken pieces. Transfer the chicken to a clay pot or casserole. Add all of the other ingredients except the chestnuts. Bring to a boil and then lower the heat under the pot to maintain a simmer for half an hour.

Stir in the chestnuts and continue simmering for another 15 minutes. This dish tastes even better if made a day ahead and the flavors are allowed to blend overnight. Reheat and serve hot over rice. This is an excellent buffet dish.

Serves 6 to 8.

MOTHER'S THANKSGIVING TURKEY

Thanksgiving, an American holiday featuring family and feast, was readily adopted by my parents. Never having cooked a turkey in China, my mother adapted her family's method of cooking goose. Her version, steaming a seasoning of fermented red bean curd, was my earliest experience with this bird—moist and succulent—accompanied by potatoes cooked in the same sauce. I thought the usual roasted turkey quite dry and tasteless in contrast to Mother's special dish. Another advantage of this steaming method is that it requires no basting.

(Illustrated opposite)

l fresh turkey, about l2-to 4 pounds
2 pounds potatoes, peeled and
    cut up if large
1 square, 2 or 3 tablespoons, of red
    fermented bean curd (nahm yuh)
1/4 teaspoon five-spice powder
1/2 teaspoon sugar
1/4 teaspoon salt
3 scallions
3 slices ginger root

Rinse the turkey and pat dry. Mix together the bean curd, five-spice powder, sugar, and salt until well blended. Rub this mixture all over the turkey inside and out. Rub the remainder over the potatoes. Place the scallions and ginger root inside the turkey.

Place the turkey and potatoes in a heatproof dish or pan which will fit inside a covered roaster or steamer. Water should be placed in the larger pot or pan, with a rack placed to keep the turkey dish above the water level.

Cover the pot and steam, checking for doneness after 90 minutes. Add more boiling water, if necessary, to keep the steamer from running dry.

This makes a centerpiece for a feast served whole with the potatoes around the turkey.

A duck or goose can also be prepared this way.

Serves 8 or more.

Above: Tania, Melinda, cousin Cathy, my sister Ann and cousin Jimmy at a family banquet during the holidays.

WINE-BRAISED CHICKEN

This classic chicken dish is named for a famous Tang Dynasty imperial concubine who was reputedly fond of wine. This tasty dish should be made with chicken thighs, legs, or wings (parts with the bones for tenderness).

2 pounds cut to up chicken
2 slices ginger root, crushed
1 clove garlic, crushed
2 scallions or 1 small leek, sliced
6 dried mushrooms, softened and sliced
  in half
2 tablespoons cooking oil
1/2 cup broth
1/4 cup rice wine or sherry
1/4 cup soy sauce
2 teaspoons sugar
1 teaspoon salt
1 piece dried orange peel, softened
1 piece cinnamon bark

Heat the oil in a wok. Stir-fry the ginger root, garlic and scallions for a minute before adding the chicken to brown.

Transfer the wok contents to a casserole or pot with the rest of the ingredients and simmer for 30 to 35 minutes or until the chicken is tender. Serve hot or cold. This dish is also excellent reheated.

Serves 4.

WINE-SOAKED CHICKEN

The Chinese usually serve this "drunken chicken" as an accompaniment to drinks, either at a wine house or as part of the preliminary toasting portion of a banquet. Accordingly, this simple dish can be prepared well ahead of time for a cocktail party buffet.

1 whole chicken or 2 whole chicken
  breasts
1 teaspoon salt
2 scallions sliced in inch pieces
2 slices of fresh ginger root, shredded
1 cup rice wine or sherry
dash of Cantonese rose wine or Madeira
  (optional)
cilantro (optional)

Cut the chicken in half for easier steaming. Rub the pieces with the salt and place in a heat-proof dish. Pour a half cup of the rice wine over the chicken and sprinkle with the scallions and ginger pieces. Steam for 20 minutes or until done. If you are using boneless chicken, reduce the time for steaming.

If possible, place the chicken pieces in a single layer in a container just large enough to hold them snugly. Strain the liquid from the steaming dish and pour over the pieces. Add the remaining half-cup of rice wine plus a dash of Cantonese rose wine. This provides a subtle flavor to the dish which can be changed by experimenting with other spirits, but this is my own variation on the usual recipe.

Allow the chicken to steep overnight, or even several days, turning occasionally. The longer the steeping, the drunker the chicken. Cut into serving pieces, retaining the shape of the original piece on the platter. Moisten with a little of the wine sauce. Garnish with sprigs of cilantro.

One chicken can easily serve 8 or more as part of a larger spread.

AUP NGUK CHAO AUH MUI
DUCK SLICES STIR-FRIED WITH PEA SHOOTS

Pea shoots are a delicacy available only seasonally and must be cooked before wilting. In this dish they are paired with roasted duck slices and fresh water chestnuts in a combination sure to delight any palate. Here is a a way stretch the enjoyment of Peking duck; after the succulent skin has been eaten with pancakes and sauce (see page 120), some of the duck meat is sliced and quickly stir-fried to create another course.

(Illustrated above)

1/2 pound roasted duck meat, sliced

1/4 pound fresh pea shoots

1/4 pound fresh water chestnuts, peeled and sliced

1 slice ginger root, shredded

2 scallions shredded

2 tablespoons cooking oil

1 tablespoon soy sauce

1 tablespoon rice wine

1 teaspoon sugar

dash of salt

dash of pepper

1 teaspoon sesame oil

1 tablespoon broth

Heat the oil in a hot wok and toss in the ginger root, scallions and fresh water chestnuts. Stir for a minute or two. Then add the duck slices with the pea shoots. Next blend in all of the seasoning ingredients and toss to mix well. Serve hot.

Serves 4 as part of a multi-course meal.

BARBECUED CHICKEN

This well-marinated chicken is an old family favorite for the summer grill. The recipe, which will serve four or more, can be expanded for a crowd.

(Illustrated opposite)

1 cut up broiler chicken
1 slice ginger root, crushed
2 cloves garlic, crushed
3 tablespoons soy sauce
2 tablespoons rice wine or sherry
2 teaspoons sugar
1 teaspoon salt
1/2 teaspoon chili oil
1 teaspoon sesame oil

Mix together the ginger root, garlic, soy sauce, wine, sugar, salt, chili oil and sesame oil. Place the chicken pieces in a bowl and pour the marinade over the chicken. Stir to cover all of the pieces, and marinate for at least an hour. Turn and baste occasionally.

Heat the coals in the grill and place the pieces to cook until done. Turn the pieces to grill evenly. The chicken can also be broiled in the oven in about 20 minutes, turning once to cook both sides.

G A H   L I H   G A I

CURRIED CHICKEN

Here is another example of Cantonese adaptation of foreign seasonings. Curried Chinese dishes are not as spicy as the Indian varieties, but show an appreciation for the subtleties of the commingled flavors of this method of spicing. Carrots may be added to this dish for color.

1 chicken, cut into bite-sized serving pieces

MARINADE:
2 tablespoons soy sauce
1 tablespoon wine or sherry
1/2 teaspoon salt
1 tablespoon cornstarch
1 pound potatoes, cut into cubes
1 onion, cut into wedges
2 cloves garlic, crushed
1/4 cup cooking oil
1 or more tablespoons curry paste
1 teaspoon sugar
1 and 1/2 cups chicken broth
1/4 cup coconut milk
1 teaspoon cornstarch

Marinate the chicken pieces in the soy sauce, wine, and salt. Then mix in the cornstarch.

Heat the oil in a wok and stir-fry the chicken to brown. Place the chicken in a casserole.

Next, stir-fry the garlic and onions, and then the potatoes, before adding these to the casserole with the broth, sugar, and curry paste. Cook for 20 minutes. Add the coconut milk, heat through, and then serve hot with rice.

Serves 4 or more.

EIGHT TREASURES STUFFED DUCK

The time-honored technique for cooking this rich, elegant dish requires long steaming of the stuffed duck, followed by deep-frying to crisp the skin. This oven-roasted version simplifies an already time-consuming process and the results are just as delicious. The finished duck, which still retains its original shape, can be quartered to serve four as a main course, or eight or more as part of a Chinese banquet. Try the same stuffing with turkey, chicken, or Cornish hens—adjusting the oven time to the size of the fowl.

(Illustrated opposite)

1 five-pound duck, carefully boned to keep the skin intact
1 cup glutinous rice, washed and soaked in 1 1/2 cups water
2 links Chinese sausage
2 ounces of cooked ham, diced
1/2 cup lotus seeds, cooked (or use diced chestnuts or ginko nuts)
1/2 cup water chestnuts, diced (or use bamboo shoots or jicama)
4 dried mushrooms, softened, stemmed, and diced

1/2 cup celery, diced
2 scallions, chopped
1 slice ginger root, minced
1 tablespoon soy sauce
1 tablespoon rice wine or sherry
1 teaspoon sugar
1/2 teaspoon salt
1/4 teaspoon pepper
1 teaspoon sesame oil
2 tablespoons cooking oil

Allow time for the stages of preparation: The duck can be boned and the stuffing prepared well ahead of time. If you cannot get the duck boned by a butcher, do your own by using a very sharp knife or kitchen shears to cut the flesh and skin away from the carcass, starting with the neck. The skin and attached meat will turn inside out as it is snipped away from the bones. Avoid piercing the skin and retain only the lower wing and drumstick bones to help keep the shape of the duck. Turn the skin side out and keep covered and cold until ready to stuff.

Cook the rice in the water for about 10 minutes, and then add the sausage to steam for another 10. Allow to cool and dice the sausage. Have the other ingredients prepared and set out near the stove.

Heat the cooking oil in a wok and cook the scallions and ginger root. Then add the celery, mushrooms, water chestnuts, lotus seeds, ham and the seasonings to stir for a minute or two. When well-blended, remove from heat and combine with the the cooked rice and sausage. Allow to cool before stuffing the duck, which should be done just before roasting.

Preheat the oven to 400 degrees. Stuff the duck by filling the upper wing and upper breast. Sew the neck opening. Fill the rest of the duck by using the lower cavity, without packing too firmly to allow for expansion, but keeping the original shape. Truss or sew the lower opening.

Place the stuffed bird breast side up on a rack in a roasting pan. Add some water to the bottom of the pan to catch the oil. Roast the duck for 25 minutes. Then lower the temperature to 375 degrees (or lower if your oven is hot) and continue cooking for another hour and 15 minutes or until done.

You may wish to make a presentation of the whole duck before cutting or the slicing may be done in the kitchen before serving on a heated and garnished platter.

CHRISTMAS DINNER WITH PEKING DUCK

For at least twenty years in my own home, I have prepared a simplified version of the oven roasted duck of Peking (Beijing).

(Illustrated Opposite)

The classic northern roasted duck is cooked without the interior sauce of the Cantonese-style fowl. The ducks are fattened by being kept in baskets for final feeding; while being readied for roasting, air is forced between the skin and the meat to ensure crispness. Such steps can be skipped by the home cook.

The crucial steps are in making certain the skin is dry before roasting and that the coating is put on to produce the rich, brown coloring and sweet, crisp taste to the skin.

We have always made the thin pancakes in which the duck pieces are wrapped for eating, and both of the girls have helped to roll and cook them over the years.

The custom has been to start the duck hanging to dry while presents are being opened on Christmas morning. Then the rest of the preparation takes place afterward.

The making of the pancakes generally takes the greatest amount of time, but with several pairs of hands helping it is easily done.

DUCK:

1 five pound duckling, preferably fresh
2 scallions
2 slices ginger root
2 tablespoons wine
1 quart water

GLAZE:

1/4 cup maltose, or honey
1 cup boiling water
2 tablespoons rice vinegar

SAUCE:

1/2 cup hoisin sauce
2 tablespoons sugar
1 tablespoon sesame oil

GARNISH:

10 scallions
cilantro (optional)

PANCAKES:

2 cups flour
3/4 cup boiling water
1/4 cup sesame oil

Above: Me slicing the duck.

Wash the duck and pat completely dry. Reserve the neck and giblets for soup or other dishes. Tie some twine around the duck so that it will hang from a hook for drying and for ease of handling.

Bring the quart of water to a boil with the ginger, scallions and wine. Holding the duck by the hanging twine, dip the duck in the water to scald, ladling the water over the duck to ensure that all of the surface has been scalded. Hang to duck in a cool place with a pan under it to catch any drips. Discard the water used for scalding.

When the skin of the duck is thoroughly dry, mix the glaze ingredients and coat the duck well with the glaze. Allow the duck to hang to dry, adding to the glaze from time to time. A fan can be used to hasten the drying process.

While the duck is drying, prepare the sauce by heating the hoisin sauce, sugar, and sesame oil together for 10 minutes. Set aside in small dishes around the table. Prepare the scallions by cutting off the white portions in two-inch lengths and slashing each end crosswise with a sharp knife to form brushes. Place in ice water to fluff the brush ends. Some of the green parts may be shredded for additional garnish.

Preheat the oven to 400 degrees. Hang the duck from the highest rack with a deep pan with water to catch any dripping fat and to prevent any fires. Or, the duck can be set on a rack which holds it upright with a catch basin for the oil.

(Continued on page 122)

(Continued from page 122)

Roast for 20 minutes and then reduce the oven to 350 degrees for another hour or so of cooking. If you have not already made the pancakes, now is the time to do it. See the following recipe.

The duck skin should be a crisp, golden brown when done. Remove carefully from the oven and slice off pieces of the skin first, in pieces about one by two inches. Then slice off pieces of the meat and arrange on platters.

The duck is eaten by placing pieces in a pancake, adding some sauce and scallion garnish and rolling up the pancake, and then enjoying the combination of crisp skin, savory sauce, and the bite of scallion pieces in the slightly chewy pancake.

MAKING THE PANCAKES:

Add the boiling water to the flour and and form a dough. Knead the dough for five minutes and then let it rest covered for 20 minutes. Knead it again to form an elastic dough. Make the dough into rolls about two inches in diameter and cut off one inch pieces. Flatten each round and brush one side with sesame oil, Stack one round on top of another with the oiled sides together.

Roll each double round into a thin pancake about five to six inches in diameter. Keep the completed

Right: Here are Melinda and I enjoying Christmas dinner at her home in California.

rounds covered as you work. When ready to cook, heat an un-oiled skillet and cook each pancake about 30 seconds on a side, or until brown spots appear on the bottom. Turn and cook the other side, and immediately separate the halves and place on a platter, which should be kept covered.

The pancakes can be made long ahead of time and refrigerated or frozen. They are reheated by steaming for a few minutes, or baked, covered in foil.

In order to balance the richness of the duck, the other dishes at the dinner should include vegetables. As there are usually extra pancakes, we make Mu Xu Vegetables (see page 146) to use up the extras. This is a recipe adapted from the better-known Mu Xu Pork dish. Other courses could include soup, appetizers, and a sweet dessert.

For this special meal, candles and a red tablecloth will brighten the scene of the holiday feast.

Serves 4 or more.

Eggs
(Gai Ahp Ahn)

EGGS

here domesticated fowl abound, eggs are a valuable by-product, so the use of this nutritious food is common in Cantonese cooking. Not only are eggs used fresh, but in the absence of refrigeration in a warm climate, ingenious methods of preservation have been developed. There are the "ancient eggs" known as Thousand-year Eggs, and salted duck eggs, which appear as appetizers or mixed in other dishes and pastries.

Eggs, as symbols of fertility and of new life, are dyed red to announce the birth of children to friends and relatives. Hard-boiled eggs, the simplest way to prepare an egg, are often embellished and flavored by crackling the shell to allow the flavoring to season the egg inside. This makes a very portable snack.

Every cook has used a quickly prepared egg dish to fill out the meal for an extra guest, and such dishes are considered above the ordinary fare if extra ingredients are added. In the past, when eggs were not so readily available on the market, eggs were considered to be the equivalent to meat.

Above: Here is a package of preserved duck eggs as they are sold in the stores. The label from a typical package is shown below. These eggs are not, of course, a thousand years old.

PRESERVED EGGS

Among the exotic novelties of Chinese cuisine is the so-called Thousand-year-old Egg, actually cured about three months in a lime pack, in which the the chemical reaction transforms the eggs into an agate-colored ovoid with a unique, mellow flavor. This is a popular appetizer and is often combined in other dishes. The preservation method used in most households for eggs is to salt them whole in brine for several weeks. Duck eggs are usually treated in this manner, and I well remember seeing crocks of salted eggs in homes of friends and relatives. Here is the simple recipe.

1 dozen eggs
1 cup salt
6 cups cool boiled water
3 tablespoons rice wine

Place the eggs in the brine and cover. Leave for several weeks. The eggs should be hard boiled before eating.

The yolks are used in Cantonese moon cakes with sweet bean filling. Mother also used them as part of the filling for glutinous rice dumplings (duhng) made for the Dragon Boat Festival in the summer.

A H N   T H L E U
EGG SHREDS GARNISH

Eggs are often made into a fluffy yellow garnish of shreds or other decorative shapes. As accompaniment to appetizer platters, noodles, mixed vegetable salads, and in mu xu dishes, these egg shreds provide both color and nutrition. This recipe uses whole eggs, but this is also a good way to use up those extra yolks left from separating whole eggs for the whites only. If only yolks are used, double the amount of broth or water.

2 eggs, well beaten
pinch of salt
pinch of sugar
1 teaspoon broth, or water
1 to 2 tablespoons cooking oil

Mix together the eggs, broth and seasonings. A skillet is best for making these eggs. Heat the skillet to moderate and cover the bottom with about a tablespoon of the oil. Pour in just enough of the mixed egg to cover the bottom with a thin layer. The temperature should not be hot enough to brown the bottom. When the egg sets, take it out and set aside to cool.

Add more oil to the skillet as needed, and continue to make thin egg rounds until all of the egg mixture is used up.

When the egg rounds are cool, roll loosely and cut into thin shreds. Other shapes can be cut from the flat rounds if you prefer. The shreds can be covered or wrapped and refrigerated until ready to use.

EGG ROLLS

These are truly egg rolls, in that the skins are made of eggs and not wheat flour. Unlike the deep-fried variety, these are steamed in a jelly-roll pattern and make an attractive design when added to a soup or casserole. Served with a dipping sauce, they make good appetizers.

They are illustrated opposite as part of the Eight Delicacies Cold Appetizer Platter. They are the items that form a complete ring, second in from the outer perimeter. Also pictures here are Braised Beef (at the top, see page 66); Soy Sauce Chicken (at the bottom, see page 101); Spicy Cold Cucumbers (in the middle, see page 154); Braised Mushrooms (on the sides, see page 149) Tea Eggs (in the center, see below) and Preserved Eggs (see previous pages). The eighth delicacy are the pickled scallions, which may be purchased, or made using our pickle recipe on page 61.

3 eggs, beaten with a dash of salt
1/2 pound ground meat
　　(I like to use pork, chicken, or veal)
1 tablespoon wine or sherry
1 tablespoon soy sauce
dash of salt
dash of sugar
dash of pepper
1 tablespoon cornstarch`
1 tablespoon oyster sauce
1 teaspoon of flour mixed in a little
water to form a paste

Using a crepe pan or skillet, add a small amount of oil and make about six thin crepes out of the beaten egg.

Mix the ground meat with the wine, soy sauce, cornstarch, oyster sauce, and the seasonings.

Cover each egg crepe with a thin layer of the meat mixture and roll each like a jelly-roll, sealing the edges with the mixture of flour and water.

Place the egg rolls into an oiled heat-proof dish and steam for 20 minutes. Slice the rolls into diagonal half-inch pieces.

I have used these as part of an appetizer platter and as one of the selections in a hot pot meal.

Serves 5 or more as an appetizer.

TEA EGGS

The marbled pattern on these eggs make them an ornamental addition to any appetizer tray, as well as a delicious snack for a picnic or packed lunch.
They are illustrated opposite as part of the Eight Delicacies Cold Appetizer Platter. They are the light colored eggs in the center, flanking a black preserved egg.

6 eggs
2 cups water
1/3 cup soy sauce
3 or 4 star anise
1 tablespoon black tea leaves

Put the eggs into a pot with enough water to cover. Hard boil the eggs and cool them off in running water. Lightly crack the eggshells all over but don't remove from the egg.

Return the eggs to the pot with the water and add the rest of the ingredients. Simmer for half an hour or more. The longer the eggs are left in the seasonings, the better the flavor.

Remove the shells to show the pretty patterning. Larger eggs can be cut into halves or quarters to serve. Use them as garnishes for other dishes, as well as part of cold platters.

THREE-COLORED STEAMED EGGS

Here is a recipe which uses three types of of eggs — fresh, salted, and Thousand-Year — in a blend that teases the palate with a variety of flavors and textures.

3 fresh eggs, beaten
1/2 cup warm broth or water
1 salted duck egg, cooked, shelled, and
    cut into small wedges
1 thousand-year egg, shelled and
    cut into small wedges
dash of sugar and pepper
2 scallions shredded
1/2 teaspoon of sesame oil mixed
    with a few drops of oyster sauce

Mix the fresh eggs with the broth, and carefully mix in the other egg slices, scallions, sugar and pepper.

Pour into an oiled, heat-proof dish and steam for 20 minutes. Before serving, drizzle the sesame oil and oyster sauce over the eggs. Serve hot.

Serves 3 to 4 as part of a meal.

HIBISCUS EGGS

The fu yeung, or hibiscus flower, is white or yellow with a hint of pink; hence, the poetic name given to this dish of shrimp scrambled with eggs. My father said that the classic dish used only the white of the eggs, which makes it a good recipe for the cholesterol-conscious. Crab meat, well picked over can be substituted for the shrimp in this dish.

1/2 pound small shrimp
4 egg whites, stirred
cornstarch

1/4 teaspoon salt
1 teaspoon rice wine
2 scallions, white parts only, chopped
1/4 teaspoon white pepper
1/2 teaspoon sesame oil
2 tablespoons cooking oil

Marinate the shrimp in a mixture of wine, cornstarch, and salt. Mix the eggs with the sesame oil and white pepper.

First stir-fry the shrimp in one tablespoon of the cooking oil until pink. Remove from wok and keep warm.

Stir-fry the white parts of scallion in the remaining oil for a few minutes before adding the egg whites. As the egg begins to set stir in the reserved shrimp and cook together for a delicately colored and flavored dish. The green parts of the scallion can be used as garnish.

Serves 3 to 4 as part of a meal.

Left: This is a hibiscus blossom, which inspired the name for Hibiscus Eggs.

STEAMED EGG CUSTARD WITH HAM

What does the resourceful house-wife do when an unexpected guest drops in for a meal? She quickly whips up a few eggs with some sea-sonings and steams an egg custard. Delicious addition or popular stand-by for family meals, these custards can be as simple as egg with a few scallions, or as elaborate as the availability of ingredients permits. Pieces of barbecued pork, mush-rooms, preserved vegetables, or dried shrimp can make this special. This version with chopped ham is one I remember my mother making.

3 eggs, beaten
3/4 cup warm broth or water
2 scallions, chopped
1 slice ham, chopped or diced
1/4 teaspoon pepper
1/2 teaspoon salt
dash of sugar
2 teaspoons oyster sauce
1/2 teaspoon sesame oil

Mix the eggs with the broth, scallions, ham, salt, pepper, and sugar. Oil a heat-proof dish and pour the mixture into it.

Place the dish on a rack in a steamer and steam for 20 minutes or until the custard is set. Sprinkle the oyster sauce and sesame oil over the custard and serve hot.

Serves 3 to 4 as part of a meal.

STEAMED EGGS WITH GROUND PORK

My sister Ann still makes this old family version of steamed egg, and she supplied this recipe.

3 ounces ground pork
1 teaspoon wine
1 tablespoon soy sauce
2 eggs
1 teaspoon ginger root, chopped fine
1 teaspoon salt
1 cup broth or water
1 teaspoon sesame oil
1 teaspoon soy sauce

Mix the ground pork with the wine and soy sauce. Beat the eggs and add the gin-ger, salt, broth and the meat mixture. Stir well and pour into a heat-proof dish.

Steam for 20 minutes or until the eggs are set. Sprinkle the sesame oil and soy sauce over the eggs and serve hot.

Serves 3 to 4 as part of a meal.

EGGS STIR-FRIED WITH SALMON

Mother used to toss together a plate of canned salmon with eggs when fresh fish was not available. I have always liked this combination of tender pink fish, crunchy onions and soft egg; however, I prefer to use leftover cooked salmon or other fish fillet in this quick dish. This recipe is enough for two as an entree or four as part of a Chinese meal.

4 eggs, well beaten
1/2 pound cooked salmon, boned and skinned
1 small onion, sliced
1 scallion, sliced
1 slice ginger root, shredded
1 tablespoon rice wine
1 teaspoon sugar
1/2 teaspoon salt
dash of pepper
2 to 3 tablespoons cooking oil

Flake the fish and prepare all the other ingredients.

Heat two tablespoons of the oil in a wok and add the ginger root, onion, and scallion to stir until flavors are released. Then add the flaked fish to blend just long enough to heat through. Remove from the wok and set aside.

Add more oil to the wok to heat. Then pour in the beaten egg and keep stirring until almost set. Add the reserved onions, ginger, and fish along with the wine and other seasonings. Stir together with the eggs and serve hot.

Serves 2 to 4 as part of a Chinese meal.

STIR-FRIED EGG YOLKS

Here is one solution to the problem of leftover egg yolks. Whip up a tasty side dish by adding some crunchy, chopped water chestnuts and seasonings to the egg.

4 egg yolks, well beaten
6 water chestnuts, chopped
2 tablespoons broth
3 scallions, chopped
1 teaspoon rice wine
1/2 teaspoon sugar
1/4 teaspoon salt
1 teaspoon sesame oil or oyster sauce
2 tablespoons cooking oil

Mix together the yolks, broth, wine, salt and sugar.

Heat the cooking oil in a wok and stir in the scallions and water chestnuts for a minute or so. Then pour in the egg mixture and stir until the egg is just set. Drizzle with sesame oil or oyster sauce and serve hot.

Serves 4 or more as part of a Chinese meal.

HOME STYLE STIR-FRIED EGGS

This typically Cantonese omelette is what is commonly called Egg Fuyung in many restaurants, except that I do not cover mine with gravy. Fresh mung bean sprouts with their delightful crunchiness are essential to the texture of this dish. Other vegetables are optional. Will serve four as part of a meal, or two as an entree.

4 eggs, beaten

1 tablespoon broth

1 cup bean sprouts with end threads removed

2 dried mushrooms, softened and shredded

1/4 cup water chestnuts, shredded

2 scallions, sliced

1/3 cup shredded cooked meat or small shrimp (optional)

1 teaspoon sugar

1/2 teaspoon salt

dash of pepper

2 tablespoons cooking oil

1 teaspoon oyster sauce

1 teaspoon soy sauce

Blend the beaten egg with the broth. Prepare the other ingredients and have everything ready for cooking.

Either a skillet or wok may be used. Heat the oil and stir-fry the mushrooms, scallions, water chestnuts, meat and bean sprouts. Add the sugar, salt and pepper. Be careful not to overcook the sprouts.

Pour in the beaten eggs and stir together until the eggs are just set. Drizzle the oyster sauce mixed with the soy sauce over the dish just before serving.

Serves 2 to 4.

Above: While leading a China tour, I purchased fresh water chestnuts for my group to sample. At home, I use water chestnuts in my stir-fried eggs.

Vegetables
(Thleu Tsoi)

VEGETABLES

Next to rice, vegetables are the most important staples in Cantonese cooking. The great profusion of greens, legumes, roots, and squashes provide to the chefs of this region the wide variety of taste, texture, and color—in addition to nutrition—in the day-to-day meals which my parents came to expect while growing up in Guangdong. Vegetable dishes were more numerous than meat entrees in most of our family meals.

More frequently, a smaller quantity of meat was used as one of the ingredients along with vegetables in a mixed dish—as a contrast in texture and flavor. This was particularly true of cured and preserved meats such as dried seafood, ham, and sausages.

Mother was faced with the challenge of fewer vegetables available in Canonsburg during the winter months; moreover, many of the American varieties were new to her. She was undaunted, and her adaptation of her native recipes and styles of cooking to these "foreign" vegetables proved so successful that her family never had to be urged to "eat your vegetables!" I have included some of her innovations in this section.

Chinese from other regions of China have told me that Cantonese seem to like their vegetables raw. They refer to the distinctive crisp-tenderness of stir-fried vegetables in Cantonese dishes. This preference for quick cooking, just enough to preserve the natural fresh flavor is possible only when one has access to young, just-picked vegetables. Then, one can indulge in the very Taoist notion of enjoying food in its natural form (short of raw). The palate can take pleasure from the highly-valued quality of "sweetness" in the plant unsmothered by heavy sauces or overwhelming seasonings. Richer flavors are more necessary when faced with older, tougher vegetables which have been stored or preserved for the winter. When we had our own garden, the just-picked vegetables made delicious and simple accompaniments to our daily fare.

The main division of vegetables used in stir-frying must be made between those that remain firm after cooking and those that soften and produce moisture in the process. In the firmer variety—broccoli, cauliflower, asparagus, jicama, green beans, carrots, etc.—a bit of chicken broth is often added to help distribute the seasonings and to aid the quick braising to finish cooking the dish. The softer leafy greens, sprouts, and the like sometimes produce extra gravy which must be thickened with a small amount of cornstarch thinned with water. Care must be taken not to have a gluey gravy, but one which is just thick enough to adhere to the pieces of vegetables to season them. Slicing of the vegetables should be uniform so that cooking of each piece is the same, and this also adds to the eye appeal of the dish.

Above: Stir-fry prep ingredients include chopped mushrooms, onions, bamboo shoots and ginger.

SPINACH STIR-FRIED WITH GARLIC

This is a very simple dish, but a very satisfying way to use tender fresh spinach. If the spinach is older, the tough stems should be removed and the leaves chopped a few times.

1 pound fresh spinach, well washed in
    several changes of water
3 cloves of garlic, minced or mashed
1 slice ginger root, minced
2 tablespoons cooking oil
1 teaspoon rice wine or sherry
1/2 teaspoon sugar
1/2 teaspoon salt

Heat the wok and add the oil. Stir in the garlic and ginger root for a minute or two to infuse the flavors into the oil.

Add the spinach, and stir to cook for a few minutes. The young spinach does not take long. Mix in the salt, sugar, and wine. Remove the spinach to a dish and serve hot.

Serves 3 to 4 as part of a meal.

HO YIU ONG THLUN THLOK MAI

BAMBOO SHOOTS, BLACK MUSHROOMS, AND BABY CORN IN OYSTER SAUCE

I like this color combination, as well as the variety of textures and the rich smooth flavor of this winter vegetables dish. It can be whipped together from one's pantry with very little preparation. When snow peas are available on the market I like to add a handful for more contrast.

Right: Commercially-prepared oyster sauce.

10 dried black mushrooms,
    soaked to soften
1/2 pound of bamboo shoots
1 can of baby corn
1 clove garlic, mashed slightly
oil for stir-frying
snow peas if available

SAUCE INGREDIENTS:
2 tablespoons oyster sauce
2 tablespoons chicken broth
1/2 teaspoon sesame oil
1 teaspoon light soy sauce
1 teaspoon rice wine or sherry
pinch of sugar
pinch of salt
pinch of pepper

Remove moisture from the soaked mushrooms by squeezing, cut off the tough stems, and cut in half if large. Drain and rinse the canned vegetables, and slice any large pieces of bamboo.

Heat one or more tablespoons of cooking oil in a heated wok and add the clove of garlic. When it begins to brown, remove the clove and discard.

Add the vegetables, including a handful of snow peas if they're in season, and stir-fry for a few minutes to cook evenly. Add the sauce ingredients and mix well. If necessary, cover and braise for a few minutes to complete cooking, especially if fresh vegetables are used.

Serves 4.

BABY BAK TSOI WITH OYSTER SAUCE

These miniature versions of the common chard/cabbage with white stems is a fairly recent addition to the array of Cantonese vegetables, but is a great favorite. I enjoy them every time I visit San Francisco. This recipe will also work with the flowering cabbage, probably the tastiest of the whole family of leafy greens.

(Illustrated opposite)

1 and 1/2 pounds of baby bak tsoi
    (bok choy) or tsoi thlim
2 cups chicken broth
2 tablespoons oyster sauce
1 teaspoon sesame oil
pinch of sugar
pinch of salt

Wash the greens carefully. If any are particularly large, cut in half lengthwise. Place them in a pot with the chicken broth and blanch until just tender, but still bright green.

Remove and arrange on a serving platter. Heat the oyster sauce, sesame oil and the seasonings with a tablespoon of the chicken broth. Pour the heated sauce over the vegetables and serve.

Serves 4.

STIR-FRIED CABBAGE

Cantonese people like head cabbage cooked just enough to remove any raw sharpness but with the pieces remaining crisp and tender. Stir-frying with a minimum of seasoning produces a simple, delicious dish which balances more savory accompaniments to a meal.

1 pound of cabbage
1 slice ginger root, mashed
1 clove garlic, mashed
1 teaspoon sugar
1 teaspoon salt
1 teaspoon rice vinegar
2 tablespoons cooking oil

Remove the tough core of the cabbage and cut the leaves in shreds less than half an inch in width.

Heat the oil in the wok and cook the ginger root and garlic to release their fragrance. The ginger root and garlic may be removed at this point.

Add the cabbage slices, along with the seasonings, and stir well to cook through. The wok may be covered for a few minutes to steam the cabbage to tender doneness. The pieces will turn a slightly deeper green. Serve hot.

Serves 4 or more.

Above: Here is the whole family in Cambridge, Massachusetts in 1957. In the back row, from left to right are Ann, mother, father and Ethel. Margaret, Jennie and I are in the front.

STUFFED BITTER SQUASH

This bumpy, green vegetable with a tail-like stem and distinctive, bitter aftertaste is not likely to enjoy wide acceptance, but Cantonese value its astringent flavor as another variation in the wide spectrum of culinary possibilities. Not all Cantonese appreciate bitter squashes, but in our home Mother's dishes using them were so good that I often feel quite nostalgic for their taste. When I visit my sister Ann in San Francisco, she makes this dish based upon Mother's recipe, but substituting minced chicken for the pork which Mother used. I even recall one time when Mother used a bit of chopped salt fish to season the pork!

(Illustrated opposite)

1 and 1/2 pounds bitter squash, 2 or 3
    depending on size
1 pound minced chicken
2 tablespoons soy sauce
1 teaspoon salt
1 tablespoon wine or brandy
1 tablespoon ginger root, chopped fine
1 clove garlic, chopped fine
1/2 cup green onions, chopped
1 cup chopped water chestnuts
    (optional)

Mix the chicken with soy sauce, salt, wine, ginger root, garlic, and green onions. Set this mixture aside to marinate while preparing the bitter squash.

Wash the squash and cut off both ends. Cut each squash crosswise into half-inch rounds. Remove the seeds and pith. Rinse carefully with cool water. If you wish to neutralize some of the bitterness, parboil the pieces for a few minutes and drain after a cold rinse.

Stuff the pieces with the chicken mixture and arrange the rounds in a shallow dish. This recipe makes enough for two eight-inch shallow dishes. Steam each dish 25 minutes, or until the meat is done. Serve warm.

Serves 4 or more.

BAMBOO SHOOTS WITH MUSHROOMS

An especially delicious variety of bamboo grows in the winter months and when coupled with dried mushrooms (called "winter" mushrooms) the dish is known as "The Two Winters." By whatever name, this is a tasty combination of vegetables for any meal.

3/4 pound bamboo shoots, sliced
8 to 10 dried mushrooms, soften,
    stemmed and sliced in half if large
1 slice ginger root, shredded
1 clove garlic, minced
2 tablespoons cooking oil
2 tablespoons soy sauce
2 tablespoons broth
1 tablespoon rice wine
2 teaspoons sugar
1/2 teaspoons salt
1/2 teaspoon sesame oil

Heat the oil in a wok and stir-fry the garlic and ginger root for a minute or so before adding the bamboo shoots and mushrooms to cook.

Combine the seasonings and add to the wok. Mix vegetables well with the seasonings. Then cover to cook over a medium fire for several minutes to absorb flavors. Serve hot.

Serves 4.

HAH MAI CHAU
PUMPKIN WITH DRIED SHRIMP

This is Mother's recipe for making use of a Halloween pumpkin. The same method can be used for any winter squash with yellow or orange flesh.

(Illustrated opposite)

1 pound pumpkin,
    cut into bite-size chunks
2 tablespoons dried shrimp, chopped
2 slices ginger root, minced
2 cloves garlic, minced
2 tablespoons cooking oil
1/4 cup chicken broth
1 teaspoon soy sauce
1 teaspoon sugar
1/2 teaspoon salt
pinch of pepper

Heat the oil in a wok and cook the garlic, ginger root, and shrimp. Add the pumpkin and toss to cook and mix.

Add the sauce ingredients, mix and cover to braise for five or more minutes, until the pumpkin is cooked.

Serves 3 to 4.

THLEU TSOI GAI
VEGETARIAN CHICKEN

With the introduction of Buddhism into China and its adoption over the centuries, the influence upon cuisine has been to provide a vegetarian specialty to the art of pleasing the palate, while satisfying the tenet to avoid eating flesh. At its most extreme, menu items which had the appearance of meat, and even almost tasted like meat became the fashion. Materials used to create these illusions included the various forms of bean curd, wheat gluten, mushrooms, nuts, root vegetables, and various seasonings. The true practitioner avoided onions, garlic, ginger root, and wine as well—all "heating" foods not appropriate for the ascetic. One example of this school of vegetarian cooking is this recipe for Mock Chicken, made from sheets of dried bean curd skin.

1 package of bean curd skin, about 6 oz.
1/4 cup mushroom soy sauce
2 tablespoons sesame oil
1 tablespoon sugar
1 teaspoon salt
6 dried mushrooms, softened
    and shredded
1/4 cup lily buds, softened and shredded
1/2 cup bamboo shoots, shredded

Right: My Canonsburg High School graduation picture.

First soften the bean curd sheets in hot water by soaking. Drain and then soak them in a mixture of the soy sauce, sesame, sugar, and salt.

Next, place the sheets on top of each other in layers. Divide the sheets into three different piles. Sprinkle a third of the shredded vegetables over the top sheet of each pile, and roll each into a flat, sausage shape.

Place the rolls into a dish and steam for 25 minutes. Slice the rolls into "chicken" pieces and serve.

Serves 4 or more.

STIR-FRIED BITTER SQUASH WITH CHICKEN

Here is another bitter squash recipe supplied by my sister Ann, who is able to buy it in San Francisco markets. The slight bitterness of the vegetable and the mild flavor of the chicken pieces is enhanced by the black bean and garlic seasoning, just as the bright green of the squash is balanced by the white of the meat. For those who find the squash too bitter, parboiling for a few minutes will make it milder, but Mother never bothered with this step!

1 and 1/2 pounds bitter squash, about 2 medium or 3 small ones
1 and 1/2 cups chicken, cut into strips (Mother used pieces cut through skin and bones)
1 and 1/2 tablespoons fermented black beans
1 tablespoon garlic, chopped fine
1 tablespoon ginger root, chopped fine
1 and 1/2 tablespoons soy sauce
1/2 teaspoon salt
2 tablespoons vegetable oil
pinch of cornstarch if necessary

Cut the squash in halves the long way. Remove the seed and pith and slice into half-inch pieces.

Mix the black beans, garlic, ginger root and soy sauce into a paste. Mother used to use the handle end of her cleaver to perform this task.

Add the oil to a heated wok. Saute the chicken pieces until just done. Remove from pan and set aside. Next, stir-fry the squash pieces until they start to turn bright green. Add the black bean mixture, rinsing out the sauce container with some water or broth and adding this to the wok. Mix thoroughly with the squash pieces and keep mixing as the reserved chicken pieces are added.

Cover and allow to simmer for a few minutes. Uncover and if the gravy is too thin, thicken with a teaspoon or more of cornstarch mixed in an equal amount of water or broth. When the gravy turns translucent, give the dish another thorough stirring before serving.

Serves 4 or more.

Above: A banquet of down-home Cantonese food in father's home village during our 1987 family tour of China. Seated, from left to right, are my friend Mary Ann, sister Ethel, myself, sisters Ann and Jennie, and fifth aunt. Standing are guides and officials.

LING NGAUH CHAU NGUK

LOTUS ROOT STIR-FRIED WITH PORK

Lotus roots are a special vegetable—the segmented lengths which grow in the soil of ponds in which the plants are cultivated. When cut, the cross sections of the roots have holes like Swiss cheese. The gossamer filaments which linger briefly between the cut surfaces are referred to in poetic metaphor as the yearning connection between parted lovers. The lotus is a plant replete with symbolism: The seeds represent fertility and the blossom purity. The roots and seeds are edible, and the leaves are used to wrap packets of rice for steaming, imparting a distinctive flavor. Both the lotus and the multipurpose bamboo are well-favored by Chinese people.

1 pound lotus root (fresh or canned), sliced with larger pieces halved
1/4 pound pork, thinly sliced
1/2 onion, sliced
3 dried mushrooms, softened and sliced
2 tablespoons cooking oil

MARINADE:
1 teaspoon soy sauce
1 teaspoon wine
1 teaspoon cornstarch

SAUCE:
1 tablespoon soy sauce
1 teaspoon sugar
1/2 teaspoon salt
1 teaspoon sesame oil
1 tablespoon broth

Place the pork in the marinade and set aside for half an hour.

Heat the oil in the wok and stir-fry the pork until the color changes. Remove and reserve.

Add a little oil, if necessary, and stir-fry the lotus root, onion, and mushrooms for several minutes. (Fresh lotus roots will take longer to cook). Add the sauce and and the reserved pork and mix thoroughly. Serve hot.

Serves 3 to 4.

(Illustrated above)

MU XU VEGETABLES

This is the vegetable version of the well-known mu xu (mu shu) pork, which can also be eaten wrapped in the thin pancakes used for Peking duck (see the recipe on page 120). It can also be served as part of a meal with rice.

(Illustrated opposite)

1/2 pound wet gluten or fried bean cake, cut in strips

1/2 cup dried lily buds, softened and the hard ends removed

6 dried mushrooms, softened, and sliced (discard stems)

1/4 cup wood ears, softened and washed

6 scallions, shredded

2 eggs beaten (may be omitted if eggs are to be avoided by vegetarians)

2 slices ginger root, shredded

1/4 pound bamboo shoots, cut in matchstick strips

1/4 pound water chestnuts, cut in strips

2 or 3 tablespoons cooking oil

SAUCE:

1 tablespoon soy sauce

1 tablespoon wine

1/2 teaspoon sesame oil

1 tablespoon oyster sauce

1/2 teaspoon sugar

1/2 teaspoon salt

2 tablespoons broth

1 teaspoon cornstarch

Prepare all of the ingredients as directed. Mix the sauce in a bowl.

Heat one tablespoon of the oil in a heated wok and stir in the beaten egg. As it begins to set, break it into strips using your spatula. Remove from wok and set aside.

Heat another tablespoon or more of the oil and stir-fry the vegetables, starting with the ginger root and scallions and adding in the rest, stirring to mix and cook. Add the sauce, mix thoroughly, and cover to cook a minute or two to heat through and blend flavors.

Add the eggs and serve hot.

Serves 4.

SPICY EGGPLANT

Mother did not prepare eggplant very often, and when she did she used the long white variety, which tasted very soft when cooked. She considered eggplant to be slightly "ouk" (toxic) and not to be eaten too frequently. I am particularly fond of the purple kind in a spicier dish, although I tend to tone down the amount of the chili pepper from the classic Sichuan recipe.

1 large eggplant, peeled and cut into cubes

1 tablespoon salt

2 cloves garlic crushed

2 slices ginger root, minced

2 scallions chopped

1 teaspoon sesame oil

2 tablespoons cooking oil

SAUCE:

2 teaspoons hot bean paste

1 teaspoon soy sauce

2 teaspoons sugar

2 teaspoons dark wine vinegar

Sprinkle the salt over the eggplant and let sit in a colander to drain for about half an hour.

Heat the oil in a wok and stir-fry the garlic, ginger root, and scallions. Add the eggplant and stir for a few minutes, until the eggplant is well cooked.

Add the sauce ingredients and mix thoroughly. Add the sesame oil just before serving.

Serves 4.

BEAN SPROUTS STIR-FRIED WITH MEAT SHREDS

Fresh mung bean sprouts are more widely available in markets, so that the tender crispness of this vegetable can be added to stir-fried dishes. Sprouts should be carefully washed and the stringy ends pinched off. Take care not to overcook them, or they'll become limp.

1/2 pound fresh bean sprouts
1/2 pound pork or chicken, cut in
   matchstick shreds
1 slice ginger root, shredded
2 scallions, shredded
1 clove garlic, minced
2 to 3 tablespoons cooking oil

MEAT MARINADE:
1 egg white
1 tablespoon rice wine
1 teaspoon salt

SAUCE:
2 tablespoons broth
1 teaspoon sugar
1/2 teaspoon salt
dash of pepper or hot pepper oil
1/2 teaspoon sesame oil
1/2 teaspoon cornstarch

Marinate the meat shreds for at least half an hour. Prepare the sprouts and drain well.

Heat the oil in a wok to a moderate temperature and stir-fry the meat shreds until the color changes. Remove the meat from the wok and set aside.

Add enough oil to make about two tablespoons and heat to high, but not smoking. Stir-fry the ginger root, scallions, and garlic for a minute or so to release flavors. Stir in the sprouts for less than a minute before returning the meat shreds with the seasoning sauce. Stir well to blend and heat through before serving immediately.

Serves 4.

JICAMA STIR-FRIED WITH PORK

A sweet, crisp vegetable which is like the water chestnut in taste, jicama is more easily peeled and may be eaten raw or cooked. This brown-skinned root is fairly common in markets now. Here is a satisfying way to serve jicama, with some meat and vegetables to add texture and taste to the dish. I like either red peppers or carrots for color.

1 pound jicama, cut in thin slices
1/4 pound pork, cut in thin slices
1 red pepper (or carrot), sliced
1 clove garlic, minced
2 scallions, sliced
2 tablespoons cooking oil
1 teaspoon sugar
1 teaspoon salt
1/2 teaspoon pepper
1 tablespoon soy sauce
2 tablespoons broth

MARINADE:
1 tablespoon soy sauce
1 tablespoon rice wine
1 tablespoon cornstarch

Marinate the meat for at least half an hour. Heat oil in the wok and stir-fry the meat until color changes. Remove from wok and set aside.

Add more oil to the wok, if necessary to make up two tablespoons. Add garlic, and scallions and stir for a minute. Then stir in the jicama and pepper slices or carrot slices to cook for a minute or two. Add all of the seasonings with the broth and blend well. Return the meat to the wok and stir to heat through. Serve hot.

Serves 4.

BAMBOO SHOOTS STIR-FRIED WITH MUSTARD GREENS

Fresh bamboo shoots are the edible products of one of China's most versatile plants. The graceful bamboo has not only been an artistic inspiration to poets and painters, but has served as raw material for furniture, baskets, baby carriages, serving utensils, carrying and fishing poles, housing, boats, and numerous other uses. The bamboo come in many varieties, but the shoots of some are culinary delicacies.

My backyard in Virginia had a stand of tall bamboo which produced many shoots after the spring rains. After harvesting the tender shoots, I would peel and parboil them for about 10 minutes in salted water with a teaspoon or so of vinegar. After draining, they are ready to use in various dishes. Here is one of my favorite combinations: the slight spiciness of the mustard greens sets off the flavor of the fresh bamboo.

1/3 pound mustard greens, chopped
    (green leaves only)
1/2 pound bamboo shoots, sliced thinly
2 scallions, shredded
1 slice ginger root, shredded
2 tablespoons cooking oil
1 tablespoon wine
1 teaspoon sugar
1/2 teaspoon salt
1/4 teaspoon pepper
1/2 teaspoon cornstarch
    mixed in 1 tablespoon broth

Heat the oil in the wok and cook the ginger root and scallions for a minute. Add the bamboo shoots and mustard greens to the wok and stir-fry for several minutes.

Add the seasonings and blend well. The sauce should be slightly thickened to cling to the vegetables. Serve hot.

Serves 4 as part of a Chinese meal.

BRAISED MUSHROOMS

These mushrooms are delicious hot or cold. I like to use them as part of an appetizer platter for a party buffet. If used cold in this manner, this recipe will serve six people.

2 dozen dried mushrooms
3-4 tablespoons cooking oil
2 tablespoons mushroom soy sauce
1 tablespoon rice wine
2 teaspoons sugar
dash of salt
1/2 cup broth
1 teaspoon sesame oil

Soak the mushrooms in hot water to soften. Rinse well, drain, and remove stems.

Heat the oil in a wok or skillet and stir-fry the mushrooms for a few minutes. Place the mushrooms in a pot with the mushroom soy sauce, rice wine, sugar, salt and broth. Bring to a boil, then lower to simmer for 25 minutes or until most of the liquid is absorbed.

Sprinkle with the sesame oil and serve either hot or cold.

Serves 6.

STUFFED MUSHROOMS

These savory steamed mushrooms can be part of a meal or serve as an appetizer.

(Illustrated opposite)

10 to 12 large fresh mushrooms,
　about 1 1/2 inches in diameter
1/3 pound ground pork or other meat
1/3 pound shrimp, chopped
5 water chestnuts, chopped
2 slices ginger root, minced
2 tablespoons onion, minced
1 tablespoon soy sauce
1 tablespoon rice wine
1 teaspoon sugar
1 teaspoon salt
1/4 teaspoon pepper
1 tablespoon cornstarch
1 teaspoon sesame oil
2 to 3 tablespoons cooking oil
cilantro (optional)

Remove stems from the mushrooms.

Mix together the ground pork, shrimp, ginger root, onion, soy sauce, wine, sugar, salt, pepper and cornstarch. Divide the filling mixture into as many portions as there are mushroom caps and pack each mushroom firmly.

Heat the oil in a skillet or wok and brown the mushrooms, filling side down. Place the mushrooms, filling side up, on a dish and steam for 30 or 35 minutes until the filling is cooked through.

Sprinkle the mushrooms with the sesame oil and garnish with cilantro before serving.

Serves 6 or more.

CAULIFLOWER WITH BLACK BEAN SAUCE

Cauliflower is another member of the cabbage family that is enhanced by the distinctive flavors of garlic/black bean sauce. Here is a quick family vegetable dish that will go with many a family meal. Try it also with the addition of some sliced pork or beef, or combined half and half with broccoli florets. If you are planning double portions for a crowd, save time by blanching the florets for a few minutes before the final stir-frying.

1 head of cauliflower, divided into florets
　with stems peeled and sliced
1 slice ginger root, minced
1 tablespoon fermented black beans,
　chopped
2 cloves garlic, minced
1 tablespoon soy sauce
1 teaspoon sugar
1/2 teaspoon salt
1 tablespoon broth
1 tablespoon cooking oil
cornstarch

Mix together the black beans, garlic, soy sauce, sugar, salt, and broth.

Heat the oil in a wok and stir-fry the cauliflower for several minutes.

Add the black bean mixture and blend well as you stir. Cover the wok for a few minutes to finish cooking the cauliflower to tender crispness, adding a little more broth if the sauce seems too dry. If the sauce is runny, thicken with a little cornstarch mixture, but this should not be necessary.

Serves 4.

FRIED BEAN CURD WITH CELLOPHANE NOODLES

Cellophane noodles are actually made from mung bean flour and are really more vegetable than grain. Here is a dish which can be served with rice as part of a meal. Mother used to make this with salty, preserved olives (lahm gok), but I find them much too salty, preferring to use dried shrimp or slices of Chinese sausage instead.

2 ounces of cellophane noodles
1 pound firm bean curd
2 tablespoons dried shrimp, or sliced sausage
4 water chestnuts, or 1/4 cup bamboo shoots
1 cup sliced Chinese flowering cabbage, or bok choy
2 slices ginger root, shredded
4 green onions, chopped
1 clove garlic, minced
cooking oil for deep-frying and stir-frying
1 tablespoon soy sauce
1 teaspoon sugar
1/2 teaspoon salt
1/2 cup broth
1 teaspoon sesame oil

Soften the noodles by soaking in warm water for 15 minutes. Cut the strands into more manageable lengths. Soak the dried shrimp, drain and set aside. If using sausage, steam and cut into slices. Cut the bean curd into one-inch cubes and deep-fry until golden brown. Drain well and set aside.

Heat about a tablespoon and a half of oil into the wok to heat. Add the ginger, garlic, and onions and stir to release flavors. Next, add the dried shrimp, water chestnuts (or bamboo shoots), and cabbage (or bok choy). Stir to mix and. Then add the soy sauce, sugar, salt, sesame oil and broth. Stir in the bean curd and noodles and mix together until the broth is absorbed. Serve hot.

Serves 4 or more as part of a meal.

COLD EGGPLANT

This is an excellent addition to a cold appetizer platter or serves as a summer side dish to any meal. Make ahead of time to allow flavors to blend.

1 pound eggplant, or several small ones
2 slices ginger root, shredded
1 tablespoon soy sauce
2 teaspoons sesame oil
2 teaspoons sugar
1 teaspoon salt
1/4 teaspoon pepper, or hot pepper oil

If the eggplant is large, remove the stem, peel, and cut into quarters lengthwise. If the eggplant are small and tender, just remove the stem and cut in halves or leave whole. Place in a heat-proof dish with the ginger root and steam for 15 minutes or until tender.

Mix the other ingredients together. Cut or tear the eggplant into pieces and pour the sauce over them. Chill and serve.

Serves 4 or more as part of an appetizer platter.

SUMMER SQUASH WITH CELLOPHANE NOODLES

My mother used to cook fuzzy squash, a Chinese summer vegetable with hairy fuzz all over, or a green gourd squash (fu lu gua) in this dish. Zucchini or yellow squash will serve as well. The contrast in textures can be augmented by including some sliced, cooked meat—roast pork, duck, sausage, or ham. However, this recipe is a vegetarian version which will serve four as part of a multi-dish meal with rice.

1/4 pound cellophane (mung bean) noodles, softened in hot water and drained

6 dried mushrooms, softened, stemmed, and sliced if large

2 scallions, sliced

1 slice ginger root, shredded

2 to 3 tablespoons cooking oil

1 teaspoon sugar

1/2 teaspoon salt

dash of pepper

1 tablespoon soy sauce

1/2 cup broth

The softened noodles can be snipped to shorter lengths for easier handling.

Heat the oil in a wok and start with the ginger root and scallions, stirring to release flavors. Then, add the mushrooms, squash, and noodles to cook in the oil for a minute or so. Pour in the seasonings, mix, adding a little more broth or water if the sauce runs dry too quickly, and then cover the wok to steam for about three minutes. All of the sauce should be absorbed. Serve hot.

Serves 4.

GREEN BEANS WITH PRESERVED BEAN CURD

In home cooking, a common seasoning is bean curd preserved in wine and salt (fu yu), also known as "wet bean cake," another by-product of the versatile soy bean. It has sometimes been called "Chinese cheese." Sold in jars, the pieces can be used alone, as a side dish salty enough to help get down a great deal of rice, or as a tasty seasoning for vegetable dishes. Try this savory flavor with spinach, cabbage, and other greens.

3/4 pound string beans, cut in 2-inch pieces

1 clove garlic, minced

1 slice ginger root, minced

2 tablespoons cooking oil

2 pieces preserved bean curd

2 teaspoons liquid from the jar (or rice wine)

1 teaspoon soy sauce

1/2 teaspoon sugar

2 tablespoons broth

1 teaspoon cornstarch mixed in 1 tablespoon water

Mash the preserved bean cakes with the jar liquid, soy sauce, and sugar. Heat the oil in a wok. Add the garlic and ginger root for a minute to cook. Then add the beans, stirring for a minute before pouring the bean cake mixture in to blend.

Pour in the broth and cover to steam the beans for several minutes, until tender, but still crisp and green. Add the cornstarch mixture to thicken the sauce, if necessary. Serve hot.

Serves 4 as part of a meal.

THLAI FUN SA LAHT
CELLOPHANE NOODLE SALAD

An excellent summer dish, suitable for picnics, buffets or cookouts, this mostly vegetable concoction can be made ahead of time. The ingredients can be varied, the meat can be omitted, and extra hot oil can be added for those who prefer more spiciness.

(Illustrated opposite)

3 ounces cellophane noodles
1/2 cup shredded cooked chicken or
    other meat
3/4 cup shredded cucumber
4 dried mushrooms, softened in hot
    water and shredded
6 water chestnuts, shredded
2 scallions, shredded
1 slice ginger root, shredded
1 tablespoon roasted sesame seeds
1/4 cup coriander (optional)

SAUCE:
2 tablespoons broth
2 tablespoons soy sauce
1 tablespoon rice vinegar
1 tablespoon lemon or lime juice
2 teaspoons sugar
1/2 teaspoon salt
dash of pepper
1 teaspoon sesame oil
1/2 teaspoon hot pepper oil

Soften the noodles by soaking in warm water for a few minutes. Then boil for three minutes until just cooked. Rinse in cold water and drain well. Cut in shorter lengths if you wish for easier serving.

Mix the noodles with all of the prepared vegetables and meat. Blend together the sauce ingredients in a bowl and pour over the salad. Stir and keep cool before serving.

Serves 4 or more.

LAHT HUANG GUA
SPICY COLD CUCUMBERS

This quick pickle is a refreshing summer side dish or addition to a cold appetizer platter. I frequently serve it as part of a buffet, but it will also pack well for a picnic without need for refrigeration.

1 pound cucumbers
1 tablespoon ginger root, shredded
1 hot pepper, deseeded and shredded
1 teaspoon salt
1 tablespoon sesame oil
2 tablespoons sugar
2 tablespoons rice vinegar
1/2 teaspoon cornstarch mixed
    in 1 teaspoon water

Peel the cucumbers, cut in half lengthwise, and deseed. Cut the cucumbers into diagonal slices. Sprinkle the pieces with the salt. Let sit for half an hour. Rinse with boiling water and drain well.

In a wok, heat the sesame oil and cook the ginger root and hot pepper shreds to release flavors. Add the sugar, vinegar and the cornstarch mixture, stirring to blend. When the mixture turns translucent, stir in the cucumber slices to mix.

Remove from heat and place the cucumbers into the refrigerator to chill.

Serves 8 or more as part of a meal.

MOLDED BEAN CURD

Here is a technique for altering the bland taste and texture of bean curd by steaming it in loquat (pei pah) shapes in Chinese porcelain spoons. This fanciful dish is light and well worth the trouble. An easier method of molding is to steam the bean curd mixture in a shallow dish and then cut the custard into petal shapes.

(Illustrated opposite)

1 pound of soft bean curd
1 egg, beaten
2 slices ginger root, minced
1/2 cup onion, chopped
1 teaspoon rice wine
dash of sugar
dash of salt
2 tablespoons cooking oil
2 scallions, sliced
1 small carrot, thinly sliced
4 fresh mushrooms, sliced
1/2 cup peas, or tender snow peas
1 ounce shredded ham (optional)
1 teaspoon sugar
1/2 teaspoon salt
1/4 cup broth
1/2 teaspoon oyster sauce
1/2 teaspoon cornstarch
   in 1 teaspoon broth or water

Mash the bean curd and mix with the beaten egg, ginger, onion, wine, and the dash of sugar and salt. Shape some of the mixture into oiled porcelain spoons (or pour into a shallow dish) and steam for 15 minutes or until set. Remove from the spoons and reserve, or cut the custard in the dish into petal shapes.

Heat the oil in a wok and stir-fry the sliced vegetables with the salt and sugar. When the vegetables are cooked through, add the broth and oyster sauce and blend well. Thicken the sauce with the cornstarch mixture and add the molded bean curd shapes carefully to avoid breaking. When the bean curd is heated through, add the shredded ham, if desired, and transfer to a warm platter. Arrange the shaped bean curd and vegetables in a pleasing pattern before serving hot.

STUFFED BEAN CURD

Variations on this tofu dish abound, with some versions pan-fried and others steamed. Stuffing ingredients also vary from region to region, but I prefer this very Cantonese recipe.

1 pound firm bean curd,
   cut into 8 triangles
2 or 3 tablespoons cooking oil
1 tablespoon oyster sauce
1 tablespoon soy sauce
1 teaspoon sesame oil

STUFFING:
1/4 pound ground meat
   (pork may be mixed with shellfish)
1 scallion, chopped
1 slice ginger root, minced
2 dried mushrooms, softened and chopped
1 tablespoon rice wine
1 tablespoon soy sauce
1 tablespoon cornstarch
dash each of sugar, salt, and pepper

Mix together all of the stuffing ingredients and blend well. Cut a slit in the long side of each triangle of bean curd and fill with two teaspoons of the stuffing, smoothing the edge. Heat the oil and brown the bean curd pieces, starting with the stuffing side. Turn to brown all sides and remove the pieces to a heatproof dish.

Pour the oyster sauce and soy sauce over the pieces and steam for 20 minutes or until the filling is cooked through. Sprinkle with the sesame oil and garnish with cilantro (optional) before serving.

Serves 4 to 6.

CHINESE NEW YEAR'S BANQUET

(THLIN NEIN)

THLIN NEIN

CHINESE NEW YEAR'S BANQUET

Every special occasion in a Chinese home calls for some special food in celebration, but the traditional festival marking the New Year—the first new moon in the old lunar calendar—is the most important event of the year in an agricultural society. The holiday falls sometime in late January or early February in our current calendar, but it continues to mark the promise of spring, and the renewal of life with hopes for greater prosperity and abundance. The celebrations used to last almost a month with days of preparation as food was purchased and cooked, for shops close for the holidays. In keeping with the idea of renewal the house is cleaned and decorated, new clothes are worn, everyone becomes a year older, and accounts are cleared so that no debts carry over into the new year.

As a child I looked forward to Chinese New Year because I knew that we would eat especially well during this festival. Mother would take time to prepare pastries and steamed puddings, golden oranges and tangerines would be piled in bowls, and Father would return from shopping with large packages of seasonal foods. As Christians, my parents did not practice the rituals of ancestor and kitchen god veneration that were part of this holiday, but they would never give up enjoying the traditional dishes and delicacies which would be eaten at the New

Year's Eve feast. It is the one time of the year when even the poorest family tries to have something special to eat, and all members try to return home to share a meal together.

Fresh seafood, in the form of a whole fish, or rare treasures of the sea—abalone, bird's nest, sea cucumber (beche de mar), or shark's fin for those who can afford it, a fine ham, duck or squab or chicken—these are some of the foods which we might have for this feast. In addition, the choicest of other ingredients in fresh or dried vegetables, nuts, and condiments would be used in the preparation of the dishes. This was the time when extra effort was spent in making a gourmet treat. Enough food would be prepared for the continuing celebrations with family and for the entertainment of guests, for even the cook gets a holiday from cooking on New Year's Day.

The holiday is also a time for friends to visit and for the exchange of gifts — usually food — among relatives and friends. Seasonal flowers — such as the flowering plum or narcissus — and colorful good luck posters and auspicious couplets add to the festive air of homes. Visitors are offered tea and refreshments: fresh and dried fruits, nuts, pastries and candies. Everyone is greeted with wishes for happiness and prosperity in the new year: "Gong Hih Fat Tsoi." I enjoyed such visits because children are given money wrapped in red paper (lai sih) by adults, including my parents. This was my own

spending money. Moreover, children were never scolded or punished during New Year's Day, for that would be a bad luck omen for the rest of the year. Likewise, one should try not to break anything, nor speak of unpleasant or evil things. Firecrackers were traditionally set off to frighten away any evil spirits.

The celebrations climaxed at the time of the full moon, on the 15th of the first lunar month, with the Lantern Festival. In many parts of China there are contests in which groups and individuals compete in making elaborate lanterns in every imaginable shape. People go out on the night of the full moon to view these lanterns, which are lit by candles, and some have moving parts kept in motion by heat from the candles. My mother marked this day by making filled round dumplings, symbolic of the full moon and togetherness, served in a sweet soup (see page 173).

When my siblings and I grew up and scattered, Mother tended to make the Christmas dinner stand in for the New Year's feast, for that was a time when most of the family members could return to celebrate together. However, the food she prepared for the laden table was traditional Cantonese festival fare. My children would get the red-paper wrapped gifts of money and be plied with sweets and dressed in red silk outfits. My parents readily adapted

(Continued on page 162)

(Continued from page 160)

American holidays to Chinese ones, especially any which provided an excuse for a feast or family get-together. The Christmas tree with its decorations added to the festive air of traditional Chinese red good luck symbols, and the giving of presents a common Chinese New Year's custom.

In my own life, I have kept the practice of celebrating the Lunar New Year with a feast of Chinese food. I have frequently entertained friends at a Chinese New Year's buffet dinner which requires careful planning and preparation. It is a challenge to provide a variety of foods which will keep on a buffet table and which allow me to entertain my guests without spending my entire time in the kitchen. The solution is to select some dishes which can be prepared ahead of time and then quickly reheated in the microwave, others which can be slow-cooked and then served hot, some which are served cold or room temperature, and only one or two that require last minute stir-frying.

This photograph of a New Year's dinner includes some dishes which can be prepared using recipes from this book. From left to right: Colorful Fried Rice (recipe on page 26), an Eight Delicacies Appetizer Platter including Soy Sauce Chicken (page 101), Braised Mushrooms (page 149), Braised Beef (page 66), Tea Eggs (page 128), Spicy Cold Cucumbers (page 154), and purchased preserved eggs and pickled scallions, Phoenix Tail Shrimp (page 92), Whole Winter Melon Soup (page 52), Eight Treasures Stuffed Duck (page 118) and Snack Walnuts (page 179) Eight is a popular number in the names of dishes because of its auspicious associations with the Eight Trigrams, the basis for ancient Divination, and the Taoist Eight Immortals, symbols of long and everlasting life.

Snacks & Sweets
(Hahm Hiem Iem Thlim)

SNACKS AND SWEETS

The Cantonese people are prolific creators of snack foods, both savory and sweet. Here in the Pearl River delta sprang up the teahouses which specialize in the tidbits known to the world as dim sum (iem thlim in our dialect of Cantonese). In Guangzhou today are establishments which boast a thousand varieties of these delectable goodies, so that the institution of having tea is a justly celebrated meal not unlike the Western brunch.

In our household, Mother produced festival and celebration savories and sweets based upon her village traditions, supplemented by Father's experience with chef's techniques from Hong Kong. Some sweets are too complex for home production—moon cakes require too many special ingredients and equipment, so they are usually purchased for holiday gift-giving. The ones which we did make at home still required

some skill to form, so that many hands are welcome in the making of these treats. My own favorite family food project was making the pastries called dim sum. I would watch as Father kneaded the dough and cut it into pieces, ready for shaping into round skins. Meanwhile, Mother mixed the fillings with pork, water chestnuts, shrimp, and her special seasonings.

Then all of us lined up to assemble the filled pork buns, and to pleat the pocket-shaped dumplings. Even the youngest girl proudly put her lopsided buns on the steamer racks. These went into the metal vat which on weekdays was used for boiling laundry starch. Soon the steam plumped the dim sum into delicious mouthfuls. We all agreed, "That starch vat gives the buns a better flavor!" None elsewhere ever tasted as good.

Left: Here I am about to eat duck-shaped dumplings in Xian, China.

HONEY GINGER PEARS

I have always been fond of the combination of ginger and pears, so I have devised this easy dessert. I had received some syrup-infused ginger in the distinctive hexagonal green jar and was thinking of ways to use it. Candied ginger can be substituted if some honey is added to enhance the flavor.

*3 pears with firm flesh,
    like Bosc or Anjou*

1 cup water

1/4 cup rock sugar, or turbinado

1 tablespoon honey

1 tablespoon sweet ginger root, minced

Peel, halve, and core the pears. Dissolve the sugar and honey in the water over low heat in a pot. Add the pear halves and the minced ginger root. Simmer the pears for about 15 minutes. Remove the pears to a serving dish.

Heat the syrup in the pot to reduce the liquid. If you wish, add a dash of pear or ginger liqueur to the syrup before pouring it over the pears. This is good either warm or cold.

Serves 4 or more.

STEAMED SPONGE CAKE

Father had a sweet tooth and was very fond of this sponge cake made the Chinese way—by steaming. If this is baked in an oven, the texture is quite different.

6 eggs
1 cup light brown sugar
1/3 cup milk
1 teaspoon vanilla or almond extract
1 and 1/2 cups all purpose flour
1 teaspoon baking powder

Left: Father rowing a boat in Boston during his visit to meet my fiancee.

Separate the eggs and beat the whites until stiff. Add sugar and continue beating. Next, combine the vanilla or almond extract, milk and the yolks and beat into the whites mixture.

Sift the flour together with the baking powder and add to the batter, mixing until well-blended.

Pour the batter into a lined and well-oiled cake pan with deep sides. Steam the cake for 25 minutes, or until a toothpick comes out clean. Remove from the pan and cool before cutting and serving.

Serves 5 or more.

ALMOND COOKIES

This type of cookies has long been associated with the Chinese, but the original was undoubtedly not baked in ovens, but pressed from ground almonds, lard, and sugar. The following recipe is closer to our notions of a proper cookie, and much less heavy. If you use your own ground almonds, use blanched ones and add 2/3 cup sugar.

1 cup shortening
1/3 cup sugar
1/2 cup almond paste
2 eggs beaten
1 teaspoon almond extract
3 cups flour
1 and 1/2 teaspoons baking soda
1/2 teaspoon salt
30 blanched almond halves

Cream the shortening and sugar. Then add the almond paste, eggs, and almond extract. Mix well.

Sift the flour, baking soda, and salt together. Add to the wet mixture and combine until you have a stiff batter.

Make a roll of the batter about two inches in diameter, and cut off half-inch rounds. Place these on a greased cookie sheet and flatten while placing an almond half in the center of each. Or you can make one-inch balls and flatten each on the cookie sheet. A beaten egg can be brushed over the tops to form a glaze. Bake in a 325 degree oven for 25 minutes.

Makes about 2 dozen.

BARBECUED PORK BUNS

These are the most popular of the filled, steamed buns produced by the Cantonese, and my favorite of the childhood homemade dim sum. The old starch vat no longer exists, but the recipe is still good. The secret of making your own is that the filling is much more generous than in the commercially made ones.

(Illustrated opposite)

BUN DOUGH:

3 cups flour
1 package yeast
1 cup of warm water
2 tablespoons sugar

Place the yeast and sugar in the warm water to activate the yeast. When it bubbles, add the flour and stir to form a dough. Knead gently for about five minutes and allow to rise in a warm place for two hours.

While the dough is rising, the filling can be made so that it will be cool for the assembly of the buns.

THE FILLING:

1 pound of barbecued pork, cut into tubes
3 scallions, chopped
1 tablespoon rice wine or sherry
1 tablespoon sugar
1 tablespoon oyster sauce
1 tablespoon soy sauce
1 tablespoon ground bean sauce
1 teaspoon cornstarch mixed with some water
1 tablespoon cooking oil

Heat the oil in a wok and stir-fry first the scallions and then the pork pieces. Add the wine, sugar, oyster sauce, soy sauce, and ground bean sauce. Mix well. If the mixture is watery, add some of the cornstarch mixture to thicken. Set aside to cool.

When the dough has more than doubled in bulk, punch it down and allow to rise another half hour. Knead it again and make into rolls about two inches in diameter. Cut into one inch rounds and flatten until the rounds are about four inches. Makes about 16 buns. They are ready to fill.

Take a dough wrapper in hand, place about two tablespoons of the filling into the middle and bring up the edges to twist together to form a

Above: Brother Tom and I when we were young.

bun. Place the bottom of the bun onto a square of parchment about 2 1/2 inches square.

Set the completed buns aside in a warm place to rise some more. When they have almost doubled in size, place in a steamer and steam for 10 or more minutes until done. Serve warm.

The buns will refrigerate or freeze. Reheat by re-steaming, or wrap in foil and bake for a few minutes.

SHRIMP DUMPLINGS

Among the dumplings which we used to steam during our family cooking projects was a savory mouthful made with a translucent dough pouch. My mother had learned to make these for village celebrations, a specialty pastry which required much skill. Her filling was a mixture of pork and shrimp, but my favorite is one that is made with large pieces of shrimp. The dough for the skin should be made fresh, for it does not refrigerate or freeze very well.

(Illustrated opposite)

Make the filling first and refrigerate while the skins are being shaped:

FILLING:

1/2 pound shrimp, cut into pieces unless small

5 water chestnuts, chopped

2 scallions , white parts only, chopped

1 egg white beaten

2 teaspoons rice wine

1/2 tablespoons cornstarch

1 tablespoon oyster sauce

1 teaspoon sesame oil

pinch of sugar and salt

When Mother used minced pork in the filling, she always cooked the mixture briefly by stir-frying to ensure thorough cooking. When shrimp is used this is not necessary. Prepare the ingredients and mix thoroughly. Keep cool before using.

DUMPLING SKIN:

(makes about a dozen):

1 cup wheat starch

(fine cake flour can be substituted)

1/4 cup tapioca starch (or cornstarch)

a pinch of salt

1 cup boiling water

1 tablespoon oil or shortening

(Mother used lard)

Combine the flours and salt in a mixing bowl. Make a well in the flour and pour in the boiling water. With a wooden spoon stir well to form a smooth dough.

Oil all surfaces before working the dough. Knead for a few minutes and form rolls about an inch in diameter. Keep covered while you work on the pieces to form skins: Cut pieces off the roll—about an inch—and flatten this round with the flat of an oiled cleaver upon an oiled board, shaping a thin circle of dough. The thinner the better, so long as the thickness is even.

When you are ready to fill the skins, take each circle and pleat half of the edge, forming a pouch. Place a teaspoon or so of the filling in each skin, and bring the unpleated edge to the pleated and pinch to seal. The shape should be able to sit on a flat surface with a curved, sealed edge on top. This is a pastry with eye appeal.

When you have prepared all of the dumplings, place them on oiled steamer trays and steam for 10 to 12 minutes. Serve hot with seasoning dips. This is a popular offering at teahouses which serve dim sum.

Above: Brother-in-law Ed with sisters Ann and Jennie at our Chinese New Year's banquet in 1998.

MOTHER'S NEW YEAR'S TARO PUDDING

The New Year's season was heralded in our home by mother's production of festival foods, of which the weightiest was the large taro pudding, from which pieces would be cut and served for many days. The custom of preparing a rich, heavy New Year's pudding (goh) grows out of the need to have something ready to feed family and relatives who gathered for reunions and friends who dropped by to offer greetings of the season. Some regional varieties used different ingredients, but most were made with glutinous rice flour and were sweet.

Mother's pudding was savory rather than sweet, and instead of the Cantonese radish-based cake, she used taros. This grayish root was sometimes boiled and eaten with some sugar on it as a snack, or braised with dried shrimp for a hearty dish. This pudding is the one I remember best as a way of cooking taro, and I have never had this particular recipe anywhere else. It may have been Mother's invention. Since taro is difficult to purchase in quantity in the United States, she often made it using some white potatoes.

1 and 1/2 pounds taro, or taro
    and potato mixed
1 cup rice flour
1 or more cups of water
2 Chinese sausages (lap cheong)
1/4 cup dried shrimp, soaked to soften
6 dried mushrooms, soaked to soften
    and stems discarded
2 scallions
1/2 teaspoon sugar
1/2 teaspoon salt
1/2 teaspoon pepper
1 tablespoon oyster sauce
1 tablespoon cooking oil

Put the taro or potatoes into a pot of water to cover and cook until done. Peel and cut into cubes.

Put the rice flour into a mixing bowl and stir in enough water to make a thick batter.

Chop the sausage, dried shrimp, mushrooms, and scallions. Heat the tablespoon of oil in a wok and stir-fry these ingredients with the seasonings until well mixed.

Add the taro and the cooked chopped mixture to the batter and stir to distribute. Pour into a well-oiled 10-inch cake pan.

Steam the pudding for about an hour. It should feel firm and a toothpick should come out clean from the center of the pudding.

Allow to cool and remove from the pan. Slice to serve. Cover with foil or plastic wrap and keep in the refrigerator. Pieces can be reheated by frying lightly.

Serves 6 or more.

Above: My mother's first passport picture.

FILLED DUMPLINGS IN SWEET SOUP

These round, glutinous rice balls are often served during the full moon after the New Year. We also had one served to us on our wedding day by the old aunties, who said that it would ensure fertility.

Right: Commercially-prepared glutinous rice powder (flour).

1 cup glutinous rice flour

1/2 cup ground sesame paste or almond paste

1 tablespoon shortening

1/2 cup sugar

Mix the ground nut paste with the shortening and sugar. Make into half-inch balls. Wet the balls and roll them in a flat pan layered with the glutinous rice flour. Keep wetting and rolling the balls to build up a coating. An alternative method is to form the flour into a dough with some water and wrap each ball with a thin wrapping. However, the rolling is the classic method.

Bring a quart and a half of water to a boil and place the dumplings in. After the water comes to a boil again, add one cup of cold water and wait for it to boil for a few minutes. Serve the dumplings in bowls with some of the broth.

Serves 4 or more.

ALMOND SOUP

This delicious drink was originally made with ground almonds mixed with rice flour and water, but this quicker version is very similar.

When I was a girl, my mother would make sweet soups which were more like creamy custards during the winter' and during the summer, cooling agar-agar gelatins and tapioca puddings. For the first full moon of the New Year, sesame seed dumplings made from glutinous rice flour in a sweet soup or plain dumplings in a savory broth were ways of marking the occasion. There are regional variations for these snacks, made from various nuts and vegetables: I have had a lotus root cream in

Hangzhou, and walnut soups, as well as red bean paste combined with ground Chinese dates in another sweet soup. In the north a common breakfast drink is almond flavored soy sauce bean milk.

The convenience of unflavored gelatin packets and canned purees of chestnuts, almonds, and the like make reproducing traditional versions of these sweet soups very easy. In the past, the labor-intensive process of grinding nuts and pulverizing dried ingredients made these rare treats in most households. Now, anyone can whip these up for a refreshing snack.

1/2 cup almond paste

3 cups water

1/2 cup milk

honey to taste

Bring the water to a boil and dissolve the almond paste in it, adding the milk to blend into a thick soup. Serve hot.

Serves 4.

FRESH FRUIT BASKET

For a summer buffet, this fruit med-ley served in a whole watermelon shell cut to resemble a basket is an attractive way to highlight the bounty of this season. Select the fresh fruits for variety in color and flavors. Canned fruits are not rec-ommended for this dish.

(Illustrated opposite)

Below: Here are Melinda and I serving a Fresh Fruit Basket on her tenth birthday.

1 large well-formed watermelon
5 to 6 pounds of fresh fruit, including
 some from each of the following:
 citrus—oranges, pink grapefruit
 (in segments without membranes)
 apples, pears—peeled, dipped in
 lemon juice, cut in pieces
 melon—honeydew or cantaloupe, in
 balls or pieces
 berries or seedless grapes
 optional—loquats, mangos, papaya,
 kiwi
1/2 cup orange juice
dash of orange liqueur

Decide how you want the melon to sit, and cut the top portion to form a basket with a handle, or simply cut off the top and serrate the edge of the melon. Scoop out the melon pulp and make into balls or pieces. Save the juice to use with the fruit.

Prepare the other pieces of fruit. You will have much more fruit than will fit back in the melon basket. Mix the fruit and fill the watermelon shell, reserving the leftover fruit in a bowl. Mix the watermelon juice and the orange juice with the liqueur, and pour half the amount over the fruit in the watermelon shell and the rest over the reserved fruit.

Serve the fruit in the melon basket, adding fruit from the reserve as needed.

Serves 8 or more.

EIGHT TREASURES RICE PUDDING

This glorified, sweet pudding is a popular banquet dish, not necessarily as a dessert, but as a festive form of rice. (Plain steamed rice is too common to complement elegant fare). The classic recipe calls for a filling of red bean and Chinese date paste. I have made it that way, which pleases Chinese dinner guests who are accustomed to the traditional flavor, but I prefer to eat my own variation with an almond paste filling. Not only is the paste easy to purchase, but I think the flavor is superior.

(Illustrated opposite)

2 cups glutinous rice
4 cups water
1/2 pound almond paste
1 teaspoon oil or shortening
1 and 2/3 cups water
3 tablespoons sugar
   (I like turbinado or date sugar)
1 tablespoons cornstarch

Also use 1 cup of assorted nuts and preserved fruits.

Select four kinds of nuts (walnuts, pine nuts, lotus seeds, gingko nuts, chestnuts, almonds, pecans, etc.) and four kinds of sugared fruits (dates, raisins, orange or citron peel, plums, cherries, kumquats, etc.).

Cut the larger pieces into strips or dice.

Cook the rice by placing in a pot with the 4 cups of water. After reaching a boil, and as the water is being absorbed, cover the pot tightly and turn the heat to low. Allow to cook without lifting the cover for 25 minutes. The cooked rice will be sticky. Traditional recipes call for the addition of lard and sweeteners to the rice, but the almond paste is sweet enough without additional sugars. A little oil added to the rice will keep it from being too sticky.

Oil a heat-proof bowl, preferably a round one large enough to hold the assembled pudding. Pack half of the rice into the bowl in an even layer, following the curve of the bowl. Place the almond paste on top of this layer of rice, leaving a rim of rice around the top uncovered. Pack the remaining rice over the almond paste, so that the filling is entirely surrounded by rice. Flatten the top of the rice.

At this point, flip the pudding onto an oiled plate by placing the plate upside down over the bowl and carefully turning the two over at the same time. You are now ready to decorate the pudding with the fruit and nuts. Starting in the center of the top, place the fruit and nut pieces in a pattern of concentric circles, alternating colors and shapes. Press the pieces into the rice a bit so that they stay in place.

When your design is completed, place the bowl carefully over the pudding and reverse the flipping process. Steam the pudding for about an hour. Before serving the pudding, prepare the syrup by combining the water, sugar, and cornstarch, stirring to dissolve completely. Bring to a slow boil until the syrup clears and thickens. Remove from heat but keep it warm by covering.

When ready to serve, flip the pudding onto a serving plate with just enough of a raised edge to hold the syrup. Pour the syrup over the pudding and serve some of it with each helping. The helpings should be in wedges to include some of the filling and the decorative pattern.

This is large enough to serve 8 as part of a Chinese meal.

BAHT THLIU PING GUO
CARAMEL APPLES

This ever-popular dessert requires quick last-minute execution. Have an oiled platter ready for the sticky-coated pieces of fruit, with a bowl or two of cold water on the side. Each diner dips the hot pieces into the water to harden the coating and cool off the pieces a little before biting into the delectable combination of crisp exterior and soft fruit. Serves six or more. Try cooking other fruits — bananas, cooked sweet potatoes, even fresh water chestnuts — using the same technique.

3 cooking apples, about a pound
2 or 3 tablespoons flour for dredging
oil for deep-frying
1 tablespoon toasted sesame seeds

BATTER:
2 egg whites
3 tablespoons cornstarch
3 tablespoons flour

SUGAR COATING:
2 tablespoons oil
1 teaspoon sesame oil
1/2 cup sugar

Peel, core, and cut the apples into thick slices. Dredge with flour.

Mix the batter ingredients until smooth. If the batter is thin, add a bit more flour.

Heat oil for deep-frying. Dip each piece of apple in the batter and fry in the hot oil until crisp and golden. Drain on paper toweling.

Heat the sugar coating until thickened and golden in color. Dip the apple pieces into the syrup to coat well, dip into the cold water to harden and place on the oiled platter. Sprinkle with the sesame seeds and serve immediately.

TSONG YIU
SCALLION BREAD

This crisp, flat bread made from a scallion flavored dough is a popular street vendor snack that is quite easy to make at home. Use them as an accompaniment to lunch with soup, or on picnics and at parties as an appetizer. This recipe will make six round breads which can be cut into wedges for serving.

2 and 1/4 cups sifted all-purpose flour
3/4 cup boiling water
1/2 cup scallions, chopped
1/2 tablespoon salt
2 tablespoons sesame oil
1/4 cup cooking oil

Place the sifted flour in a bowl. Make a well in the flour and pour in the boiling water slowly while stirring with bamboo chopstick or wooden spoon. When all of the flour is dampened and a ball of dough is formed, place the dough on a floured surface and knead for five minutes until smooth and elastic. Cover and let rest for 20 minutes.

Divide the dough into six portions. Work on one portion at a time. Roll each portion flat, to about 1/4 inch. Brush the top surface of the dough sheet with sesame oil. Then sprinkle with 1/6 of the salt and scallions. Roll the sheet tightly jelly-roll style, into a long rope, tucking in the edges to keep in the filling. Coil the rope of dough tightly into a round and tuck in the end. Cover and set aside while making the other breads in similar fashion.

When all six are done, flatten each with a rolling pin into a round, flat shape of about a half inch or less thickness. The thinner you roll the bread, the crisper the end result.

Heat about two tablespoons of oil in the bottom of a flat skillet and brown the breads on both sides, adding more oil to the pan as needed. The breads should be golden and crisp. Cut into wedges and serve warm. They can be made ahead of time and reheated in a moderate oven before serving.

SNACK WALNUTS

These seasoned walnuts are wonderful for cocktail snacks or for use as a crisp garnish. Tour groups I have taken to China enjoyed them there, and I have experimented with preparing my own versions. Try the same seasonings and methods of preparation with pecans. Leftovers can be stored in a tightly covered container.

2 cups shelled walnut or pecan halves, (about 1/2 pound)
1 cup water
1/4 cup date sugar or sucanat
3 tablespoons maltose or honey
1/4 teaspoon salt
dash of pepper
oil for deep frying

Blanch the nuts in boiling water and drain. Remove excess brown husks.

Place the sugar, maltose, salt and pepper in the cup of water and bring to a boil.

Add the nuts to the syrup and simmer for 15 minutes to allow the nuts to absorb the flavorings. Drain the nuts and let cool.

Heat the oil in a wok to moderate high and fry the nuts to a golden brown. Be careful not to burn the nuts. Drain well and allow to cool and crisp.

SNACK WALNUTS: REDUCED FAT METHOD

A lower calorie technique for preparing these nuts is to follow the same recipe as above, but instead of deep-frying place the nuts on a baking sheet in a single layer in a moderately hot oven (375 to 400 degrees) and roast for 10 to 12 minutes. Stir once or twice during the roasting.

FIVE SPICE SNACK WALNUTS

An entirely different flavor is obtained with the following seasonings added to the nuts, which are then roasted in the oven.

2 cups blanched walnuts or pecans
1 tablespoon brown sugar
1/4 teaspoons salt
dash of pepper
1/2 teaspoon five spice powder

Combine the seasonings and toss the nuts in the mixture to coat. Place the nuts in a single layer on a baking sheet and drizzle or spray with a little oil. Bake in a 375 or 400 degree oven for about 10 to 12 minutes, stirring to expose all sides. Allow to cool and serve at room temperature.

Left: Four cousins in San Francisco for Christmas in 1973. Cathy, Melinda and Tania are in the back row, with Jimmy in the front.

DEEP-FRIED WON TON

A popular cocktail treat, these crunchy tidbits must be kept and served hot to stay crisp. Offer a choice of dipping sauces with the won ton. I have included both a sweet-and-sour and a hot mustard dip. This recipe produces two dozen won ton.

(The completed recipe is illustrated opposite, while the photograph below shows commercially available square won ton wrappers)

2 dozen 3 and 1/2-inch square won ton wrappers (pictured below)

FILLING:

1/4 pound ground pork (or other meat)
1/4 pound shrimp, chopped
1/4 cup chopped water chestnuts
1 slice ginger root, minced
1 scallion, chopped
1 tablespoon soy sauce
1 tablespoon rice wine or sherry
1 teaspoon sugar
1/2 teaspoon salt
1/4 teaspoon pepper
oil for deep-frying

Combine the pork, shrimp, and water chestnuts with the rest of the filling ingredients.

Make the won ton by placing a heaping teaspoon of the filling on each wrapper. Fold the filled wrapper into a triangle. Seal by pressing the layers of dough together around the filling. Bring the side points together and press together, sealing with a little water to form a cap shape. Cover the finished won ton to keep moist while you are making the rest.

Heat the oil to a temperature of 375 degrees to deep-fry the won ton until golden brown. Fry a few at a time to avoid them sticking together. Drain well on paper towels. If necessary, keep in a warm oven until ready to serve.

The dips described below right are excellent with fried won ton.

SWEET AND SOUR DIPPING SAUCE:

In a saucepan combine 3 tablespoons rice vinegar, 1 1/2 tablespoons sugar, 2 tablespoons plum sauce, 1 teaspoon minced lemon zest, and 1/2 teaspoon cornstarch dissolved in a teaspoon of water. Simmer until blended and slightly thickened. If the consistency is still too watery, add more cornstarch mixture. Cool to room temperature to serve.

HOT MUSTARD SAUCE:

Blend together powdered mustard with an equal amount of water. A small amount of cooked oil or sesame oil poured on the mustard adds to the flavor. Warn your guests of the spiciness of this mustard.

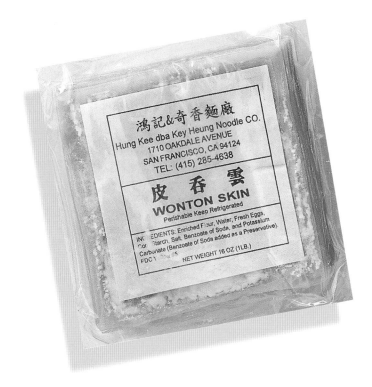

GAI LUHNG
SWEET FRIED CRESCENTS

These deep-fried dumplings are a rich combination of chewiness, sweetness, and crunchiness. Mother used to make them for special occasions, using peanuts, coconut shreds, and sugar in the filling. Glutinous rice flour accounts for the chewiness of the dough. My preference for filling includes walnuts and chopped dried fruit with candied citrus. This recipe makes about a dozen crescents.

(Illustrated opposite)

FILLING:

1/4 cup shredded coconut
1/4 cup chopped apricots
1/4 cup chopped walnuts, or peanuts
1 tablespoon chopped, candied orange
    peel or citron
1 tablespoon sugar
1 teaspoon sesame seeds

Mix the filling ingredients in a bowl and set aside while preparing the dough for wrapping the crescents.

WRAPPING:

1 1/2 cups glutinous rice flour
2 tablespoons all-purpose wheat flour
1 teaspoon baking powder
1 teaspoon sugar
1 tablespoon shortening
3/4 cup hot water

Combine the flours with the baking powder and sugar. Make a well in the dry ingredients and place the shortening in it before pouring in the hot water. Mix with a wooden spoon to form a dough. Knead the dough a few minutes until smooth. Roll the dough into a sausage shape and divide into a dozen pieces. Each piece should be pressed and formed into a round wrapper about 1/4 inch thick. Place about a tablespoon of the filling in each wrapper and fold in half to make a crescent. Crimp the edges to seal.

Heat oil in a wok to about 350 degrees for deep frying. Put only a few crescents into the oil at a time and cook for a few minutes until golden. Drain well and serve warm.

HAP HAU CHA
WALNUT TEA

Reputedly good for skin, nails, and hair, walnut soup has long been a favorite drink for Chinese women, especially on wintry evenings. Blenders or food processors make the grinding process so much easier so that this "tea" can be enjoyed at any time.

1 cup shelled walnuts
1/4 cup rice flour
1 quart water
1/2 cup rock or light brown sugar
dash of salt

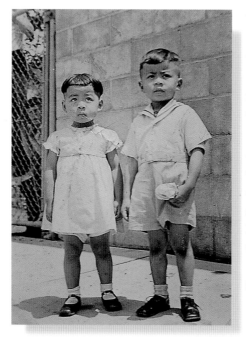

Above: Brother Tom and I in Canonsburg.

Pour enough boiling water over the shelled walnuts to cover for 10 minutes to blanch. Remove the light brown inner skin and allow the nuts to dry. Roast the nuts in a single layer in the oven. Grind the nuts to a fine powder in the blender.

Add the ground walnuts to the quart of water in a pot. Add the rice flour, sugar, and salt and bring to boil to dissolve. Lower heat to simmer for about 20 minutes. Pour into individual bowls to serve hot.

Serves 4 or more.

TARO DUMPLINGS

A favorite in Cantonese teahouses, this rich and satisfying treat can be made at home as well. The southern taro root comes in various sizes, with the larger ones best for this pastry. Sweet potato may be substituted for the taro, but lacks the latter's flavor and smooth texture. This recipe will produce a dozen dumplings, excellent as an appetizer or part of a meal. Make extra quantities for freezing and reheating in a hot oven.

1 pound taro root
1/3 cup wheat starch (gluten-free flour)
1/2 cup boiling water
1/2 teaspoon sugar
1/2 teaspoon salt
3 tablespoons shortening
oil for stir-frying and deep frying

FILLING:

2 tablespoons dried shrimp, softened and chopped (or use chopped ham)
4 dried mushrooms, softened and minced
1/4 pound chopped meat (pork, chicken, beef)
1 slice ginger root, minced
1 scallion, chopped
1 tablespoon rice wine
1 tablespoon tablespoon
1 tablespoon soy sauce
1 teaspoon oyster sauce
1 tablespoon broth
dash of sugar and salt

Peel the taro, cut up and boil in water to cover for half an hour, or until soft. Drain and mash the taro while still warm until smooth, discarding any hard pieces.

While the taro is cooking, assemble the prepared filling ingredients. Heat about 2 tablespoons oil in a wok and cook the chopped meat until the color changes. Add the ginger root, scallion, dried shrimp, and mushrooms. Stir for a minute or so before adding all of the other seasonings. When the liquid is all absorbed, remove the filling from the wok and allow to cool.

Pour boiling water into the wheat starch, salt, sugar and shortening and mix to form a soft dough. Combine with the mashed taro and knead the mixture together until smooth. Roll into a cylinder and divide into 12 pieces. Flatten each piece into an oval about half-inch thick. Place a tablespoon or more of the filling into each oval and fold over, pinching the edges to seal and forming a football-shaped dumpling. Continue to make all of the dumplings in the same manner.

Heat oil to at least 365 degrees for deep-frying in the wok. Add the dumplings a few at a time to the hot oil. The dumplings are done when they turn golden brown. Remove with a mesh sieve and drain well. Serve warm.

Makes 12 dumplings.

Above: Three sisters, Jennie, myself and Ann.

RECIPE NOTES

RECIPE INDEX

GENERAL INDEX

*Following pages:
Much of San Francisco's
Chinatown still looks like
it did when mother and
father bought their store
here in 1957.*